TECHNICAL
REPORT

Security Cooperation Organizations in the Country Team

Options for Success

Terrence K. Kelly, Jefferson P. Marquis,
Cathryn Quantic Thurston, Jennifer D. P. Moroney,
Charlotte Lynch

Prepared for the United States Army

The research described in this report was sponsored by the United States Army under Contract No. W748H-06-C-0001.

Library of Congress Cataloging-in-Publication Data

Security cooperation organizations in the country team : options for success / Terrence K. Kelly ... [et al.].
      p. cm.
   Includes bibliographical references.
   ISBN 978-0-8330-4911-7 (pbk. : alk. paper)
      1. Security Assistance Program. 2. Security, International. 3. International cooperation. 4. Military planning—United States. 5. United States—Military policy. I. Kelly, Terrence K.

UA12.S383 2010
355'.0320973—dc22

2010002726

The RAND Corporation is a nonprofit research organization providing objective analysis and effective solutions that address the challenges facing the public and private sectors around the world. RAND's publications do not necessarily reflect the opinions of its research clients and sponsors.

RAND® is a registered trademark.

Published 2010 by the RAND Corporation
1776 Main Street, P.O. Box 2138, Santa Monica, CA 90407-2138
1200 South Hayes Street, Arlington, VA 22202-5050
4570 Fifth Avenue, Suite 600, Pittsburgh, PA 15213-2665
RAND URL: http://www.rand.org/
To order RAND documents or to obtain additional information, contact
Distribution Services: Telephone: (310) 451-7002;
Fax: (310) 451-6915; Email: order@rand.org

Preface

Security assistance, as it is currently in law and practice, reflects an approach that is adequate in a stable environment in which efforts can be planned, resourced, and executed without major changes, but not sufficiently agile for a world in which challenges are more dynamic and flexibility is essential for success. To address this issue, the U.S. Army asked RAND to do a "quick turn" assessment of security assistance and propose alternatives for improving it. This technical report is the result of that project.

This research considers the missions and structure of security assistance organizations in U.S. Missions around the world and presents three options for improving the functionality of security assistance organizations based on best practices and what is known about the tasks they are likely to take on. This project was undertaken as a quick-turnaround study for the Army's Office of the Deputy Chief of Staff for Operations and Plans. The research took place from February to April 2008, with some adjustments based on input from Headquarters, Department of the Army, and from reviewers after this period ended.

This research was sponsored by MG David Fastabend, Director of Strategy, Plans, and Policy, Office of the Deputy Chief of Staff, G-3/5/7, U.S. Army, and conducted as part of RAND Arroyo Center's crosscutting research efforts. RAND Arroyo Center, part of the RAND Corporation, is a federally funded research and development center sponsored by the U.S. Army.

The Project Unique Identification Code (PUIC) for the project that produced this document is DAMOC09192.

The project point of contact is Terrence Kelly, 412-683-2300, ext. 4905, tkelly@rand.org.

For more information on RAND Arroyo Center, contact the Director of Operations (telephone 310-393-0411, extension 6419; FAX 310-451-6952; email Marcy_Agmon@rand. org), or visit Arroyo's Web site at http://www.rand.org/ard/.

Contents

Figures

Tables

Summary

The United States conducts a wide range of security cooperation missions and initiatives that can serve as key enablers of U.S. foreign policy efforts to assist and influence other countries. For a relatively small investment, security cooperation programs can play an important role by shaping the security environment and laying the groundwork for future stability operations with allies and partners.

Security cooperation,[1] in the form of noncombat military-to-military activities, includes "normal" peacetime activities, such as building the long-term institutional and operational capabilities and capacity of key partners and allies, establishing and deepening relationships between the United States and partner militaries, and securing access to critical areas overseas. Security cooperation also can include conducting quasi-operational efforts, such as helping U.S. partners and allies manage their own internal defense.

However, current national security challenges both create significant demands for U.S. security cooperation programs and deplete the resources needed to carry out these missions. The wars in Iraq and Afghanistan are occupying the regular, reserve, National Guard, and Special Forces trainers and advisors who would normally be called on to train and advise military counterparts. Furthermore, U.S. allies, who often complement the efforts of U.S. advisors and trainers, are also stretched thin by their own deployments to Iraq and Afghanistan.

In an effort to find ways to improve security cooperation planning, coordination, and execution, the U.S. Army's Office of the Deputy Chief of Staff for Operations and Plans asked RAND Arroyo Center to conduct an assessment of key facets of U.S. security cooperation—specifically, the missions, capabilities, and structure needed in the security assistance organizations (SAOs)[2] that coordinate the military aspects of U.S. foreign relations, including security cooperation activities, at U.S. Missions around the world.

Challenges Exist at All Three Levels of U.S. Security Cooperation

In its assessment, the RAND research team identified three levels of players that plan, coordinate, execute, and oversee U.S. security cooperation efforts. However, a number of challenges exist at each level that can inhibit the effectiveness of SAO efforts.

---

[1] In this context, "security cooperation" includes both security assistance (Title 22 U.S. Code) and security cooperation (Title 10 U.S. Code).

[2] Although SAO is sometimes used as an abbreviation for *security assistance officer*, we do not use it as such in this report.

Washington, D.C., Level

At the federal government level in Washington, D.C., anywhere from thousands to billions of dollars are allocated for security cooperation efforts in a given country through various programs. Executive Branch agencies, particularly the departments of Defense and State, work together to ensure that funds are allocated according to the wishes of Congress and the President. At the same time, Congress plays a pivotal role in these processes through its annual authorizations and appropriations bills, as well as its oversight and approval of the statutory framework that governs security cooperation.

At this level, two main funding authorities govern security cooperation:

- **Title 22** funds are appropriated to the State Department, which often transfers them to DoD, which in turn manages and executes most security assistance programs. Title 22 includes Foreign Military Sales programs. Title 22 is less flexible in some ways, mainly because Congress authorizes and appropriates these funds on a by-country and by-program basis, and requires congressional notification and permission to move funds from one effort to another.
- **Title 10** funds are appropriated to DoD and are intended for operations and maintenance of the U.S. military. These funds are often used to fund international participation in U.S. joint exercises, military personnel exchanges, or military-to-military contacts as a way to enhance the relationships between partner militaries and U.S. forces.

Because of the differences in funding authorities for Title 10 and Title 22, there is a general separation between the two, resulting in distinct organizations and cultures and leading to stovepiped approaches to working with foreign countries.

Regional Level

At the next level in the military chain of command are the Regional Combatant Commands (RCCs) and the service component commands that support them. The RCCs play a critical role in guiding military manpower and resources via their regional strategic planning processes to the country team at the U.S. Mission, and they also play a significant role in developing regional security cooperation objectives, particularly the judgments they make about the requirements to build complementary partner capabilities.

Organizationally, DoD and the State Department are not well matched to develop or coordinate policy. The State Department has no organization equivalent to the RCCs because ambassadors and country teams answer directly to the State Department in Washington. Therefore, while the State and Defense departments coordinate policy at the headquarters level in Washington, they coordinate less often and in an ad hoc fashion in the regions, which is where DoD actually crafts the bulk of its security cooperation plans.

Country Level

At the country level, each U.S. Mission has a country team that includes representatives from many federal agencies, as well as the key players from the departments of Defense and State, all under the direction of the U.S. ambassador. The members of the country team, which includes the SAO, must coordinate their efforts both in country and with their home agencies to successfully deliver U.S. assistance, including security cooperation.

However, given the restrictions on Title 22 funding, ambassadors have no authority to move money among different security cooperation activities or accounts, which greatly restricts the SAO's ability to tailor security cooperation during a given year should the need arise. In addition, most SAOs frequently have only a handful of military personnel to arrange and execute complicated and delicate security cooperation activities.

Changes Are Needed to Improve Security Cooperation Effectiveness

The RAND research team found that organizations that currently manage U.S. security cooperation work relatively well in most countries where peacetime engagement is the norm. In particular, current practices and authorities suffice if security cooperation efforts can be planned in advance and there is no need for significant change during a given budget year. However, when unbudgeted requirements arise, whether they are for new programs or for significant changes to existing programs, the current system has trouble working within inflexible authorities and funding mechanisms and what is, at times, less-than-ideal interagency coordination.

To help DoD and the State Department overcome these hurdles, the RAND team developed three options that could help improve SAO capabilities and capacity:

Option A: Improve Efficiency

This option focuses on improving the functions of the current country-level SAO during normal peacetime engagement by capturing and implementing best practices. Because it requires changes in procedures only, it could be implemented through DoD policies and directives. These improvements in coordination and cooperation could be made immediately without any changes in authorities, structure, or staffing. Improving efficiency would include three principal elements:

Institutionalize vertical integration. To implement vertical integration for security cooperation, agencies in Washington, D.C., need to be able to work as a team, which could help integrate security cooperation policy and resources. Vertical integration would also provide reachback support to the country team and the regional players, as needed. The RCC and its service component commands would play critical roles in this process through its support of the country team and the SAO. The experiences of "Team Ukraine" offer a good example of vertical integration.

Institutionalize horizontal integration. Horizontal integration requires the establishment of functional working groups within the country team. This approach, in turn, would enable SAOs to cooperate with multiple military efforts as well as civilian agencies. To do so, security cooperation personnel in country would need the skills to understand the larger goals of U.S. foreign policy and civilian agency partners. The experiences of SAOs in the Philippines and Thailand offer good examples of horizontal integration.

Improve security cooperation training for Defense Attaché Office personnel. Another potential improvement would be to better educate all defense personnel within a country team on the security cooperation roles and responsibilities of the SAO and the defense attaché's office. This enhanced understanding can help improve the country team's ability to most effectively manage relations with the host nation's military.

xiv Security Cooperation Organizations in the Country Team: Options for Success

Option B: Increase Flexibility

This option considers long-term legislative and funding changes that are needed to increase the SAO's flexibility to perform its security cooperation functions. In particular, this option recommends three principal steps that could be taken to more rapidly implement changes to authorities when needed.

Grant additional authorities. Given the abundance of restrictive authorities that govern U.S. security cooperation efforts, it would be a positive step if Congress passed legislation that would allow country teams to respond to "emergency" circumstances in the national security arena with prompt, flexible U.S. security cooperation missions (specifically, missions that do not require the introduction of a U.S. Joint Task Force) in support of allies and acceptable partners. This legislation could be based on the Stafford Act,[3] which permits the federal government to respond quickly to a domestic disaster. Congress should carefully define what criteria constitute an actionable emergency in order to control what programs are permitted under what conditions. The new authority could allow the ambassador or security assistance officer to

- move funding from one program category to another
- provide equipment and supplies
- conduct training on nonlethal techniques
- conduct training on lethal techniques
- conduct broader security-force training and provide advice and assistance.

To be viable, the statute would need well-defined conditions under which the President could declare a need for each type of activity, as well as prompt reporting requirements to the Congress.

Prepare "pocket" legislation. If Congress does not provide additional authorities that enable more-flexible security cooperation efforts, DoD can, in coordination with congressional staff, research and prepare draft legislation that would provide the flexible authority and funding needed if an emergency situation arose. This "pocket" legislation would be ready to be submitted for a vote as soon as possible in the event of an emergency situation that requires a rapid U.S. response.

Prepare "pocket" executive orders. Similarly, another step would be to examine the inherent powers of the President to delineate what the President can do without congressional approval in situations in which U.S. national security is threatened by actions abroad. If the presidential powers are deemed sufficient, DoD could draft standby executive orders that the President would activate, and delegate those powers when additional flexibility and funding are needed for particular security cooperation activities.

Option C: Shape and Assist

Currently, no single DoD official controls all military elements involved in security cooperation activities in most countries. Authority varies depending on the country, the function that is being performed, and the organization that is performing the function. To better integrate all the security activities and players within a country, this option seeks to give the senior

---

3 Robert T. Stafford Disaster Relief and Emergency Assistance Act, Public Law 93-288, as amended, 42 U.S.C. 5121–5207, November 1988.

defense official (SDO) at the U.S. Mission additional authority over all security cooperation and train, advise, and assist (TAA) efforts in that country.

This option would not be appropriate for most countries. However, for select countries of high importance to the United States that are facing significant threats, it could be a critical element in U.S. national security efforts. Although Option C could stand alone, it would be most effective if it builds on Options A and B.

Under this option, the SDO would be responsible for and direct most military personnel in country—all except those operating directly under a combatant commander—using a staff that would be capable of managing a full TAA effort. The SAO should also include military personnel who possess the ability to act with great political sensitivity, who have a good understanding of U.S. foreign policy goals in their country and how military efforts fit within this framework, and who are experienced in the execution of advisory and assistance missions.

Because the SDO works for the ambassador, putting the SDO in charge of these activities would make the ambassador responsible for all activities that do not fall explicitly under a combatant commander. The SDO would have the ability to request, accept, and manage out-of-country assets and also to coordinate with special operations forces and intelligence agencies, as necessary. The SDO also should have the ability to hand off security cooperation and TAA efforts to an RCC.

Implications for the U.S. Army

Our research shows that the Army should play a central role in most of these proposed changes. As the service with the largest and most formal training and preparatory roles in security cooperation, the Army is a natural choice to either formally lead (e.g., as executive agent) or provide intellectual leadership in the realm of policy proposals and idea generation. In particular, should Option C be adopted, the Army would need to create a way to supply trainers, advisors, and direct assistance personnel. The Army can also help to develop a regional joint and interagency organization that can accept the incoming supply of DoD personnel and tailor teams that will in turn support the embassy and the partner nation.

Acknowledgments

The authors would like to acknowledge the contributions of several people, without whom this report would not have been possible. First, MAJ John LeMay of the U.S. Army, who oversaw this effort for Headquarters, Department of the Army. His guidance and input were invaluable. Brigadier Simon Wolsey of the British Army, Major LeMay's boss at the inception of this project, also provided valuable guidance. In the course of this effort, we consulted with many subject matter experts, too numerous to name. However, of particular importance were David Gompert of the RAND Corporation; COL (retired) Robert Killebrew; COL Kevin D. Saderup, U.S. Army; and Celeste Ward, Deputy Assistant Secretary of Defense for Stability Operations (now at RAND).

Additionally, thanks go to Thomas Szayna of RAND and COL (retired) William Flavin of the U.S. Army's Peacekeeping and Stability Operations Institute, who provided rigorous and helpful reviews. Their comments and insights made this report a better document.

Abbreviations

APEP	Administrative & Professionals Exchange Program
ASCC	Army Service Component Command
CMEP	Civil-Military Emergency Preparedness (program)
CoESPU	Center of Excellence for Stability Police Units
COIN	counterinsurgency
COM	Chief of Mission
CORDS	Civil Operations and Revolutionary Development Support
CTFP	Counter-Terrorism Fellowship Program
CTR	Cooperative Threat Reduction
DAO	Defense Attaché Office
DATT	defense attaché
DIA	Defense Intelligence Agency
DoD	Department of Defense
DMC	Defense and Military Contacts program
EIPC	Enhanced International Peacekeeping Capabilities
ELN	National Liberation Army (Colombia)
ESAF	El Salvadoran Armed Forces
FAA	Foreign Assistance Act
FAEP	Foreign Academy Exchange Program
FARC	Revolutionary Armed Forces of Colombia
FID	foreign internal defense
FLO	foreign liaison officer
FMF	foreign military financing
FMLN	Farabundo Marti National Liberation Front
FMS	foreign military sales
GPOI	Global Peacekeeping Operations Initiative
GTEP	Georgia Train and Equip Program
IMET	International Military Education and Training

INCLE	International Narcotics Control and Law Enforcement Program
INL	International Narcotics and Law Enforcement
JTF	joint task force
JUSMAG	Joint U.S. Military Assistance Group
MAAG-V	Military Advisory Assistance Group, Vietnam
MACV	Military Assistance Command, Vietnam
MILGRP	military group
MPEP	Military Personnel Exchange Program
MTT	military training team
NCO	noncommissioned officer
NGB-SPP	National Guard Bureau–State Partnership Program
ODC	Office of Defence Cooperation
OEF-TS	Operation Enduring Force–Trans Sahel
OSD	Office of the Secretary of Defense
PKO	peacekeeping operations
P.L.	Public Law
PPI	Proliferation Prevention Initiative
RCC	regional combatant command
RUE	Reciprocal Unit Exchange
RVNA	Republic of Vietnam Armed Forces
SAO	security assistance organization
SATMO	Security Assistance Training Management Organization
SC/TAA	security cooperation/train, advise and assist
SCC	service component commands
SCO	security cooperation organization
SDO	senior defense official
SOF	special operations forces
SOP	standard operating procedures
SPP	State Partnership Program
TAA	train, advise, and assist
TDY	temporary duty
TEP	Train and Equip Program
TTPs	tactics, techniques, and procedures
USAID	U.S. Agency for International Development

CHAPTER ONE

Introduction

The U.S. military must plan for a wide range of security cooperation[1] missions, ranging from "normal" peacetime security cooperation activities—such as building the long-term institutional and operational capabilities and capacity of key partners and allies, establishing and deepening relationships between the U.S. and partner militaries, and securing access to critical areas overseas—to managing quasi-operational efforts, such as managing foreign internal defense within the overall foreign policy objectives of the United States. Security cooperation, in the form of noncombat military-to-military activities, is a useful part of the military's toolkit in conflict prevention.[2] Although security cooperation requires a relatively small investment with respect to the overall efforts of the U.S. military, it can be a key enabler of the success of future U.S. military missions by shaping the environment and laying the groundwork for future coalition and stability operations with allies and partners.[3]

Current world conditions both create significant demands for U.S. security cooperation programs and deplete available resources to carry out these missions. The wars in Iraq and Afghanistan are occupying the regular, reserve, National Guard, and Special Forces trainers and advisors who would normally be called on to train and advise military counterparts. Furthermore, U.S. allies, who often complement the efforts of U.S. advisors and trainers, are also stretched thin by their own deployments to Iraq and Afghanistan.

It is important to consider the context in which security cooperation takes place. Security assistance and cooperation are only components of U.S. efforts to assist and influence coun-

---

[1] According to Headquarters, Department of the Army, *Security Force Assistance,* FM 3-07.1, May 2009, para 1-15:

> *Security Cooperation* is all Department of Defense interactions with foreign defense establishments to build defense relationships that promote specific U.S. security interests, develop allied and friendly military capabilities for self-defense and multinational operations, and provide U.S. forces with peacetime and contingency access to a host nation (JP 3-07.1). Finally, security cooperation occurs across the spectrum of conflict and is not exclusively a peacetime activity.

[2] See Joint Chiefs of Staff, *Department of Defense Dictionary of Military and Associated Terms,* Joint Pub 1-02, June 9, 2004, for definition of "security cooperation":

> All DoD interactions with foreign defense establishments to build defense relationships that promote specific U.S. security interests, develop allied and friendly military capabilities for self-defense and multinational operations, and provide U.S. forces with peacetime and contingency access to a host nation.

[3] See Headquarters, Department of the Army, *Operations,* FM 3-0, February 2008; and Department of Defense, "Military Support for Stability, Security, Transition, and Reconstruction Operations," DoD Directive 3000.05, November 28, 2005; and also Department of Defense, *Quadrennial Defense Review Report,* February 2006. A number of recent guidance documents suggest that "peacetime" engagement through security cooperation will become a larger part of the military's toolkit in shaping operations. See William S. Wallace, "FM 3-0 Operations: The Army's Blueprint," *Military Review,* March–April 2008.

tries. Security assistance[4] is a subset of the larger foreign assistance effort that includes such programs as bilateral and multilateral economic assistance, humanitarian assistance, and law enforcement assistance. Furthermore, all these programs support U.S. policy goals that are generally targeted at moving countries politically toward democracy and economically toward market economies. In other words, it is important to view security cooperation as one element of U.S. foreign policy and specifically as a key contributor to targeted efforts that involve both political and military components to help nations address their security and how it is managed. Although the exposition of these goals and the tools used to achieve them change from one presidential administration to the next, their fundamental orientation generally does not. Thus, security assistance and cooperation must be structured in ways that contribute to these larger goals.

In addition, there is an important distinction between the command relationships for a security cooperation mission and those for combat or other operations (e.g., stability operations). Under U.S. law, combat operations must be conducted under a chain of authority that flows from the President, through the Secretary of Defense and a combatant commander, to U.S. forces on the ground, often led by a Joint Task Force (JTF) commander. In contrast, it is the U.S. ambassador's responsibility to manage, on behalf of the President and the Secretary of State, relations with the host nation as the point person for U.S. foreign policy, of which security cooperation is one part. The security assistance officer,[5] as a staff section within the country team, helps manage the military aspects of these relations. This makes sense from a policy perspective because the ambassador is responsible for U.S. relations with the host nation government—even with its security elements. However, in circumstances in which large U.S. military units are participating with the host nation government in combat or other significant operations, the primacy of the responsibility for relations with the host nation military will often shift to the commander of a large deployed military force.

Analytical Objectives and Approach

To better understand the missions and structure of security assistance organizations (SAOs) in U.S. Missions around the world, as well as consider options for improving SAO functionality, the Army's Office of the Deputy Chief of Staff for Operations and Plans asked RAND Arroyo Center to undertake a quick-turnaround study that would address these issues. In particular, the RAND study team was asked to focus on one part of the larger security

---

[4] According to FM 3-07.1, para 1-19,

> "Security Assistance is a group of programs authorized by the Foreign Assistance Act of 1961, as amended, and the Arms Export Control Act of 1976, as amended, or other related statutes by which the United States provides defense articles, military training, and other defense related services by grant, loan, credit, or cash sales in furtherance of national policies and objectives (JP 3-57). Security assistance is a specific subset of security cooperation and may focus on external or internal threats."

Note that security assistance programs, though often implemented by the U.S. Defense Department, are funded and overseen by the U.S. State Department.

[5] Although SAO is sometimes used as an abbreviation for *security assistance officer*, we do not use it as such in this report.

cooperation/train, advise, and assist[6] (SC/TAA) problem: the capabilities and capacity needed in an SAO at the country level.[7] In its assessment, the RAND research team identified three levels of players that plan, coordinate, execute, and oversee U.S. security cooperation efforts. The team also identified a number of challenges at each level, which can inhibit the effectiveness of the SAO's efforts.

Washington, D.C., Level. Executive Branch agencies, particularly the department of Defense (DoD) and the Department of State, work together to ensure that funds are allocated according to the wishes of Congress and the President. At the same time, Congress plays a pivotal role in these processes through its annual authorizations and appropriations bills, as well as its oversight and approval of the statutory framework that governs security cooperation.

Regional Level. At the next level in the military chain of command are the Regional Combatant Commands (RCCs) and the service component commands that support them. The RCCs play a critical role in guiding military manpower and resources via their regional strategic planning processes to the country team at the U.S. Mission, and they also play a significant role in developing regional security cooperation objectives, particularly the judgments they make about the requirements to build complementary partner capabilities. However, DoD and the State Department are not well matched organizationally to develop or coordinate policy.

Country Level. At the country level, each U.S. Mission has a country team that includes representatives from many federal agencies, as well as the key players from the departments of Defense and State, all under the direction of the U.S. ambassador. The members of the country team, which includes the SAO, must coordinate their efforts in country as well as with their home agencies in order to successfully deliver U.S. assistance, including security cooperation. However, ambassadors have no authority to move money between different security cooperation activities or accounts, which greatly restricts the SAO's ability to tailor security cooperation during a given year should the need arise. In addition, most SAOs frequently have only a handful of military personnel to arrange and execute complicated and delicate security cooperation activities. Furthermore, while the SAO reports to the respective RCC, most U.S. agency representatives at the embassy take direction from the ambassador and also report to their parent agency.[8]

In its analysis, the RAND team reviewed several different kinds of SAOs that have worked to handle a wide range of challenges at the country level; discussed the challenge with knowledgeable, serving security assistance officers, academics, and other experts; reviewed examples of legal authorities from other disciplines that could be adapted to fit the security cooperation

---

[6] The U.S. military is now using the term *Security Force Assistance*—the definition of which is still under debate. This document will continue to use "TAA."

[7] Following Defense Institute for Security Assistance Management (DISAM) practice, we use SAO as the generic name for all such organizations. Other names, such as Offices of Defense Cooperation, Joint U.S. Military Assistance Groups, and other such country- or region-specific names, will be used only when referring to specific organizations that use that name. Furthermore, this report does not provide an overview of the status quo because it is adequately addressed in the DISAM *Green Book*.

[8] According to Joint Publication 3-08,

> "The ambassador is the personal representative of the President to the government of the foreign country or to the IGO to which he or she is accredited and, as such, is the COM, responsible for recommending and implementing national policy regarding the foreign country or IGO and for overseeing the activities of USG employees in the mission. . . The ambassador has extraordinary decision making authority as the senior USG official on the ground during crises." (p. II-18)

efforts; and adopted an approach that identified successes from the past and challenges for the future. Based on this input, RAND developed three options that incrementally increase SAO capabilities and capacity:

- **Option A, Improve Efficiency,** focuses on improving the functions of the current embassy level organization during "normal" peacetime engagement by capturing and implementing best practices.
- **Option B, Increase Flexibility,** focuses on changing or adding authorities and funding mechanisms to provide more nimble capabilities to the embassy team.
- **Option C, Shape and Assist,** focuses on improving the capability of the SDO's country team staff to manage security assistance efforts in country as a quasi-operational head-quarters (short of commanding troops in combat).

These options are addressed in detail in the following chapters.

The methods used in this analysis combine a review of the pertinent literature, good practices taken from selected current and historical security cooperation efforts, lessons from programs or statutes that address similar problems in other fields, and discussions with experts and practitioners in the field.

Study Parameters

Ideally, a thorough effort at examining the issue of improving U.S. provision of security assistance would include a formal assessment of existing capabilities, posit a defendable set of requirements, identify a capability and capacity gap, and make recommendations to fill that gap. To accomplish these objectives within the time frame set for this study, the RAND team relied heavily on previous research done over several years for the Army, the Office of the Secretary of Defense (OSD), and the Air Force. The RAND team also reviewed several different kinds of SAOs that have worked to handle a wide range of challenges at the country level; discussed the challenge with knowledgeable serving security assistance officers, academics, and other experts; reviewed examples of legal authorities from other disciplines that could be adapted to fit the security cooperation efforts; and adopted an approach that identified successes from the past and challenges for the future. Based on these, the RAND team developed the three options described previously that incrementally increase SAO capabilities and capacity.

Organization of This Report

Building on the overview presented in this chapter, Chapter Two discusses, in depth, the challenges of coordinating security cooperation initiatives at each organizational level. Each of the subsequent chapters examines the three options introduced above: Chapter Three focuses on ways to improve efficiency; Chapter Four focuses on increased flexibility; and Chapter Five focuses on improving shape and assist efforts. Chapter Six presents an overview of the findings and recommendations.

CHAPTER TWO

Understanding the Challenges of Security Cooperation Coordination

Successful delivery of security cooperation depends on all levels of the government working together. The country team consists of many U.S. agencies under the direction of the U.S. ambassador that must coordinate their efforts in country as well as with their home agencies in order to successfully deliver U.S. assistance, including security cooperation. The country team can include such agencies as the U.S. Agency for International Development (USAID), the Departments of Justice, Treasury, Commerce, and Agriculture, and many others in addition to the representatives from the departments of Defense and State.

The country team does not ensure unity of effort. Above the country level in the military chain of command are the RCCs. The RCCs (and the military service component commands that support them) play a critical role in guiding military manpower and resources via their regional strategic planning processes to the SAO as part of the country team. While the RCCs are generally viewed as implementers of national strategic guidance, they also play a significant role in developing regional objectives for security cooperation. This is particularly important because of their ability to make regional judgments about requirements to build complementary partner capabilities. The RCCs therefore play a critical role in coordinating and integrating many policies and programs that include efforts by service headquarters and the Office of the Secretary of Defense (OSD) and sometimes with other agencies in Washington, D.C. Furthermore, the Regional Combatant Commander or his designate evaluates the SAO, not the ambassador.[1] This creates the potential for conflicting guidance and loyalties.

Congress, through its annual authorizations and appropriations bills and through the establishment of the statutory framework that governs security cooperation and assistance, plays a pivotal role in these processes. Executive Branch agencies work together to make sure that funds are allocated according to the wishes of Congress and the President. Through program managers, anywhere from thousands to billions of dollars are allocated in a given country by means of various security cooperation programs.

Main Challenges

Many structural challenges at each of the three levels make security cooperation difficult.

---

[1] DISAM, *Green Book*, p. 4-15.

Washington, D.C., Level

At the Washington level, there are two main funding authorities related to security assistance and security cooperation, Title 22 and Title 10. Title 22 funds are appropriated to the State Department, which often transfers them to the Defense Department, which in turn manages most security assistance programs.[2] In addition, foreign military sales (FMS) programs, which are funded by the foreign government, also fall under Title 22.

Title 10 funds are appropriated to DoD and are intended for operations and maintenance of the U.S. military. For example, Title 10 funds often are used to fund international participation in U.S. joint exercises, military personnel exchanges, or military-to-military contacts as a way to enhance the relationships between the world's militaries and 'U.S. forces. By law, at least 50 percent of the benefits of programs funded under Title 10 must accrue to the U.S. military.

Because of the differences in funding authorities for Title 10 and Title 22, there is a general separation between the two. As a result, each has generated its own organizations and cultures, leading over time to stovepiped approaches to working with foreign countries.

Some generalizations may be made about the programs operated under these two authorities. The Title 22 system is less flexible than Title 10 in important ways, mainly because Congress authorizes and appropriates these funds on a by-country and program basis, so that moving funds from one country or program to another requires congressional notification and permission. Furthermore, unlike DoD, which produces a multiyear funding program tied to its long-term plans, the State Department has a single-year focus, which makes it very difficult to plan over the long term or change plans once they are authorized and funded.[3] Furthermore, related programs, even if planned by the SAO, are often managed by agencies in Washington that do not coordinate their efforts. For example, foreign military financing (FMF) may be used to fund defense services for foreign militaries,[4] but it is not coordinated with the International Military Education and Training (IMET) program, which sends foreign military personnel to the United States or DoD schools for training and education. The end result of single-year focus and stovepiped program management is a limited ability of State and Defense officials to oversee and synchronize all of the security cooperation activities being conducted with foreign militaries.

In contrast, Title 10 funds, as long as they are used for the operations and maintenance of the military, can be moved fairly easily among programs if Congress is notified and other restrictions placed on DoD Title 10 security cooperation programs are adhered to. Many of the restrictions placed on Title 10 funds prohibit the military from training foreign forces, so the majority of security cooperation programs focus on information exchanges and exercises that include both U.S. military and foreign forces.

Another challenge at the Washington level is the great disparity in manpower and funding between DoD and the State Department. Because the State Department's security assis-

---

[2]   For a complete discussion of Title 10 and Title 22 authorities, as well as a general description of security cooperation and security assistance, see the DISAM *Green Book* Web page, undated.

[3]   Changing such plans often requires notifying Congress and getting its permission. Because the State Department does not produce a multiyear program, long-term planning is not coordinated between it and its oversight and funding committees in Congress.

[4]   According to the Arms Export Control Act, Section 23, Foreign Military Financing is used to "finance the procurement of defense articles, defense services, and design and construction of services by friendly foreign countries."

tance workforce has far fewer people than DoD has, it has difficulty coordinating with all of the major DoD players (e.g., the RCCs). For example, it is simply impossible for State Department Political-Military Bureau personnel to respond to every invitation to participate in military exercises, conferences, and meetings, which is where a great deal of security cooperation coordination is accomplished.

The military service headquarters oversee their own institutional support to the plans developed by OSD (e.g., the Guidance for the Employment of the Force), the Joint Staff (the National Military Strategy), and the RCCs (theater campaign plans). The service component commands (SCCs) connect the services and the RCCs, but the services also provide security cooperation assistance from service agencies (e.g., the Security Assistance Training Management Organization [SATMO] at the U.S. Army Training and Doctrine Command).

Regional Level

The SCCs are often located in their regions and staffed by individuals familiar with those regions (including active-duty reservists and National Guard personnel). Because they answer to both their service headquarters and the RCCs, the SCCs are sometimes caught between guidance issued by both. Furthermore, SCCs have limited staffs for planning and executing security cooperation activities and virtually no staff for assessing the effectiveness of the vast number of events they conduct on behalf of the RCC and the services. As a result, they frequently take the role of program executors, with long-term planning and evaluation occurring in other parts of the overall security cooperation system.

Organizationally, DoD and the State Department are not well matched to develop or coordinate policy. In particular, the State Department does not have an operational equivalent to the RCC in every region. The regional bureaus at the State Department provide policy guidance to embassies but usually do not operate major programs.[5]

Furthermore, State Department regions and RCC areas of operation are not aligned. State Department functional bureaus (e.g., International Narcotics and Law Enforcement [INL]), which tend to be more operational than regional, also differ substantially from RCCs. In particular, they typically manage contracted programs rather than conduct them using government employees. These bureaus operate more like elements of OSD than like an RCC in this regard. Although guidance to a particular embassy is coordinated within the State Department—and often with the National Security Council, DoD, and other departments—before it is sent out, it goes directly from Washington, D.C., to the affected country rather than through an RCC-equivalent organization. Furthermore, while the military relies heavily on the RCC to craft regional plans and fund regional efforts, the State Department does not possess the organization, manpower, or resources to coordinate fully with the six RCC staffs. Therefore, while the State and Defense departments coordinate policy in Washington, they coordinate less and in an ad hoc fashion in the regions, which is where DoD actually crafts the bulk of its security cooperation plans.

---

[5] Functional bureaus at the State Department do operate programs. For example, the Bureau of International Narcotics and Law Enforcement oversees law enforcement programs for country teams. However, the regional bureaus "own" the embassies.

Country Level

Congress determines Title 22 security assistance funding based on the President's budget submission, usually by program and by country. Funding cannot be moved among programs or activities without congressional approval. In particular, ambassadors have no authority to move money among accounts or activities, which greatly restricts the embassy's ability to tailor security cooperation during a given budget execution year should the need arise. In 2006, the State Department's Director of U.S. Foreign Assistance devised a plan that would allow ambassadors to move money within a handful of strategic "accounts," but the plan was shelved because of the enormous difficulty in crafting the requisite legal authorities.[6] Interagency pushback may also have played a part in foiling this effort.[7] DoD and other agencies were reportedly worried that the ambassador would control their funding sources under this plan and that they would have little control over long-term planning and execution of programs that had historically been the responsibility of DoD and other agencies.

Security assistance officers frequently have only a handful of military personnel to arrange and execute complicated and delicate security cooperation activities. DoD responsibilities in the embassy are conducted primarily by the SAO, which executes Title 22 and Title 10 programs with the host nation, and the Defense Attaché Office (DAO), which reports to the Defense Intelligence Agency (DIA).[8] Furthermore, while most U.S. agencies at the embassy take direction from the ambassador, they also report to their home agencies.[9] The SAO, for example, is evaluated by the RCC chain of command. Therefore, coordination and cooperation at the country team level is often dependent on the personalities of the officials stationed there, and on the managerial prowess of the ambassador and deputy chief of mission to guide the disparate agencies and personnel co-located at the embassy.

Foreign Internal Defense

According to Joint Publication 3-05 (p. II-7), foreign internal defense (FID) involves the "participation by civilian and military agencies of a government in any of the action programs taken by another government or other designated organization, to free and protect its society from subversion, lawlessness, and insurgency." This mission can take place in the context of either large or smaller conflicts. It is often conducted by special operations forces and in countries to which the United States provides security cooperation, but it is not usually supervised

---

[6] For a good description of the recent history in changing existing authorities, see Noam Unger, "Foreign Assistance Reform: Then, Now, and Around the Bend," *InterAction*, July 2007.

[7] For example, see Senator Robert Menendez, "U.S. Foreign Assistance Under the Microscope at Senate Hearing," press release, June 12, 2007.

[8] DoD Directive 5105.75, *Department of Defense Operations at U.S. Embassies*, December 21, 2007, establishes the position of Senior Defense Official, who shall be the diplomatically accredited defense official in an embassy. This could be the traditional defense attaché or the security assurance officer. Implementation is still ongoing. In many countries, the DAO also has some security cooperation responsibilities.

[9] In a worst-case situation, the ambassador can direct any U.S. official to leave the country, and so could cause the SAO to be removed. However, this would be an extraordinary occurrence.

by the SAO. The relationship between security cooperation, security assistance, and foreign internal defense (FID) is depicted in Figure 2.1, taken from FM 3-07.1.[10]

We revisit aspects of the concepts presented in this figure in Chapter Five, in which we talk about command and control relationships between security cooperation efforts and other efforts in a country, including FID.

Focus on Organizational Responsibilities of DoD Staff at Embassies

As described briefly above, DoD representation at the embassy level is split between the SAO (led by the security assistance officer) and the Defense Attaché Office (DAO) (led by the defense attaché). These positions may be filled by any of the services, and are often tailored to the type of military assistance provided: air, naval forces, or Army. However, in a recent effort to streamline DoD activities at the embassy level, DoD Directive 5105.75 (December 2007) requires that one of these officers, either the security assistance officer or defense attaché, also act as the senior defense official (SDO). This will provide one single point of responsibility for defense efforts on the country team. A number of additional requirements would contribute to the SDO's ability to manage security cooperation in ways that would also further the country team's efforts at security sector reform as well as address more comprehensively the host nation's needs and appropriate U.S. responses. These requirements include the following:

Figure 2.1
Security Cooperation, Security Assistance, and Foreign Internal Defense

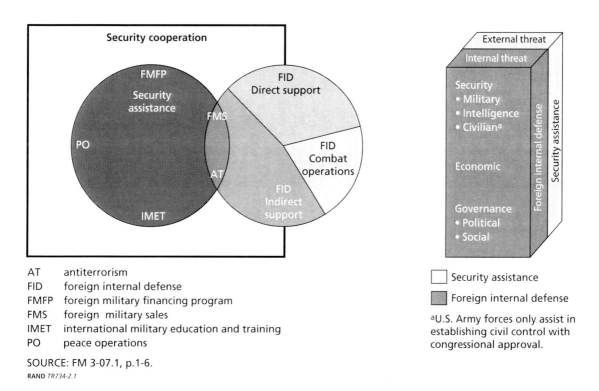

AT   antiterrorism
FID   foreign internal defense
FMFP foreign military financing program
FMS   foreign military sales
IMET international military education and training
PO   peace operations

SOURCE: FM 3-07.1, p.1-6.
RAND TR734-2.1

☐ Security assistance
■ Foreign internal defense

aU.S. Army forces only assist in establishing civil control with congressional approval.

---

[10] Headquarters, Department of the Army, *Security Force Assistance,* FM 3-07-1, May 2009.

- assessing host-nation security-sector needs for rule of law, human rights, humanitarian assistance, defense reform, and military capabilities
- providing logistical support for outside military teams coming into the country
- coordinating civilian-military support and/or events
- helping coordinate stability operations
- conducting regional and bilateral exercises
- coordinating and/or supporting U.S. training in the host nation.

Note that some of these functions are already conducted by other offices in an embassy or by agencies on a country team. For example, State Department or USAID officials on the country team already monitor human rights, humanitarian assistance, and the rule of law. Rather than duplicate these existing capabilities, the SDO could cooperate with these other agencies and perhaps augment and deepen their capabilities.[11]

We next discuss the options outlined in Chapter One.

---

[11] How the country team approaches the political and military tasks necessary to achieve overall U.S. policy objectives, in addition to determining the appropriate roles of each agency, is an important issue that is under consideration in several parts of the U.S. government. A comprehensive answer to this question is important but beyond the scope of this report.

CHAPTER THREE

Option A: Improve Efficiency

The first of the three options focuses on improving SAO efficiency at U.S. Missions. Because they require changes in procedures only, these improvements in coordination and cooperation could be implemented through DoD policies and directives without any changes in authorities, structure, or staffing. These recommended improvements are based on successful and innovative U.S. practices that have been demonstrated in Ukraine, Georgia, Thailand, and the Philippines.

As noted in Chapter One, the current set of authorities, structure, and practices can work well in normal, peacetime efforts in which program budgets are part of the normal budget cycle. This permits the SAO and its counterparts at the RCC and in Washington to plan and execute a suite of programs that meets U.S. needs as well as those of the host nation. An SAO's ability to do this is enhanced by improving its ability to coordinate and cooperate with the entire host of actors across agencies and at the three levels of government introduced in Chapter One (Washington, regional, and country team).

Institutionalize Coordinating Mechanisms

How can the security cooperation improvements outlined above be best achieved? One way is to better link all levels of effort in which an SAO works—from Washington, D.C., to the embassy. To illustrate, we look first at the organizational structure used in "Team Ukraine" (see the case study in Appendix A). It offers useful lessons from the work that was done in focusing U.S. government assets in a "normal," peacetime environment on helping to rebuild the Ukrainian military. In this example, OSD and European Command country teams, consisting of regional desk officers and policy officials, worked together with the State Department, Intelligence Community, and other key government partners to create a "virtual network" of policy planners. This working group operated at all levels—from Washington, D.C., through the RCC, and down to the SAO on the country team. It operated virtually through most of the year but met several times a year in conjunction with already existing conferences, such as the European Command's Theater Security Cooperation Working Group, to craft a living security cooperation plan for Ukraine. This informal working group successfully wove together the embassy, RCC, and Washington levels and helped the Ukrainian government develop a good approach to security sector reform. However, Team Ukraine lost its effectiveness as the people involved moved out of their positions, and the lessons learned for creating a successful security cooperation organization were lost.

The Georgia Train and Equip Program (GTEP), which was created shortly after the Team Ukraine effort, built on the Team Ukraine model and involved some of the same institutional players (e.g., OSD's Eurasia Office). This is further noteworthy because the demands placed on the GTEP by agreements reached in 1999 by President Bill Clinton and Georgia President Eduard Shevardnadze were to be fulfilled inside of an already budgeted time frame, requiring the difficult task of rebudgeting within the cycle. This was successfully done, although the fact that it had presidential level interest was surely helpful in making it happen.

These two efforts were successful because entrepreneurial actors in various agencies from Washington to the country team worked together to coordinate and collaborate. Although an important element of this effort was coordination among different agencies in Washington, a key aspect was the integration achieved between Washington and the country team, as well as the host nation. We refer to this aspect of improved coordination and cooperation as *vertical integration.*

The next model, based on U.S. experiences in Thailand and the Philippines, provides an example wherein formal efforts at organization at the country team level can greatly facilitate coordination and cooperation within the group of actors working to support a host nation.

Functional Working Groups at the Embassy Level

Improvements can also be achieved within the country team at an embassy. To achieve this, the SAOs at U.S. embassies need to institutionalize functional working groups of main stakeholders at the embassy level in an effort to improve in-country coordination as well as the reachback capabilities of the SAO, primarily because all players in country have agreed to an approach and communicate this to their home agencies.

A good example of this concept is used in the Philippines (see Appendix A). Functional working groups at the embassy level weave together those U.S. officials working on behalf of their agencies. For example, the counterterrorism working group incorporates a wide range of stakeholders, including the FBI, the departments of Homeland Security and State, and a host of other offices, in addition to DoD. Agreeing on approaches at the country team level permits the country team to speak with a single voice to parent organizations in Washington about needs and progress. This, in turn, helps to coordinate various funding, authorities, and activities, with the aim of moving toward collaborative or shared end states more efficiently. Because this practice requires cooperation beyond merely the DoD in-country component, it is an important step forward that we will touch upon again in Chapter Five, where we consider an option designed to provide the capabilities and capacity needed for a full range of TAA missions. In particular, it has important implications for the country team's ability to help the host nation align the management of its security and its security institutions with best practices and international law.[1] We refer to this approach as *horizontal integration.*

Cross-Training on SAO Duties for the DAO

Finally, another potential improvement entirely within DoD's authority is to better educate all defense personnel within a country team on the roles and responsibilities of the SAO and the DAO. A strict definition the security cooperation roles played by each may be counter-

---

[1] Note that fostering such host-nation political-military efforts will be a true country team enterprise, extending beyond the role of the SAO. Security assistance officers should be key players in these efforts, even though they will probably not oversee them.

productive and would limit the flexibility of the SDO and ambassador to manage defense efforts within the country team. However, our interviews indicated that a lack of understanding between the SAO and DAO on the respective security cooperation roles of each, as well as what some perceive as a misallocation of duties, can hurt the county team's ability to most effectively manage relations with the host nation's military. While we see no reason to mandate one solution and thus remove flexibility from personnel at a given embassy, we do see a need for those who man the DAO to be familiar with the duties of the SAO, since DAOs often perform some security cooperation duties.[2]

Implications of Option A: Improve Efficiency

The recommendations that make up Option A focus mainly on improving coordination and cooperation of military and civilian staff already on the ambassador's team, at the regional level, and in Washington. Recall that Option A calls for three categories of changes that could be accomplished without additional resources of authorities. They were characterized as vertical integration, horizontal integration, and cross-training of DAO personnel in security cooperation skills. The U.S. government could implement any of these separately, but it would achieve better results if it implemented them all concurrently.

To implement vertical integration, agencies in Washington need to be able to work as a team that would integrate policy and resources in the capital. It would also provide reachback support to the country team and regional players as needed. The RCC and Army Service Component Command (ASCC) would play a critical role in vertical integration through its regional integration and country team support roles. This would include developing tactics, techniques, and procedures (TTPs) or standard operating procedures (SOPs) on how to support the SAOs in the region, as well as its current planning responsibilities. The ASCC, as the regional Army headquarters, would also integrate Army efforts with the SAO.

Horizontal integration requires the establishment of functional working groups within the country team. This, in turn, requires the ability to cooperate with multiple military efforts as well as civilian agencies. To do so, security cooperation personnel in country (and DAO personnel in certain circumstances) will need the skills to understand the larger goals of U.S. foreign policy and civilian agency partners.

Cross-training of DAO personnel to perform SC/TAA functions should be a straightforward effort, although it will affect professional development and rotational schedules. This is particularly important for senior DAO personnel who might fill the role of the security assistance officer in country.

Implementation of these changes requires two efforts. To succeed, the military will need to identify and institutionalize the good practices required for vertical and horizontal integration and will need to develop doctrine and concepts that facilitate their being put to use. We have provided a starting point for this effort with our discussion of Team Ukraine, the GTEP program and the Joint U.S. Military Assistance Group (JUSMAG) functional teams in Thai-

---

[2] The training of security assistance officers is an important issue. To contribute well to their ability to help with larger political-military issues, this training should include not only processes but also political-military concepts. We recommend that such training be the subject of a future study.

land and the Philippines. However, such changes need to be made rigorously and maintained over time.

Implementing these changes comprehensively would require an interservice and interagency effort. However, the Army could make much progress on its own in those embassies where it runs the SAO function and by participating in DoD and interagency working groups to move this agenda forward.

The implications of these changes are summarized in Table 3.1 for ease of reference. The columns in the table present the level at which changes could be implemented (column one) and four critical functions in which changes might occur. The actions represented by entries in these columns would not all need to be implemented for progress to be made, but as noted above, more progress would be made with a comprehensive approach.

Summary

Option A: Improve Efficiency, has three principal elements:

- Institutionalize vertical integration—i.e., coordination measures that connect U.S. agencies in Washington to each other, to the RCC, and to the country team, using methods similar to Team Ukraine.
- Institutionalize horizontal integration—i.e., coordination measures in the country team on key functional areas similar to those used in Thailand and the Philippines.
- Improve security cooperation training for DAO personnel.

Table 3.1
Implications of Option A: Improve Efficiency

Level	Organization	Manpower	Training	Doctrine
Washington, D.C.	Interagency security cooperation teams in Washington, D.C.		Training for security cooperation personnel in all services and agencies	Joint and interagency doctrine and concepts related to security cooperation and political-military aspects of reform
Army	Capture and institutionalize security cooperation lessons learned		Training for some interservice/interagency personnel	
Region	Interagency regional security cooperation focus	Interagency staff available to RCC	More interagency involvement in exercises with a security cooperation/FID dimension	
ASCC	Develop capability to participate in vertically integrated security cooperation efforts		Train ASCC personnel in security cooperation	TTPs and SOPs for assisting SAOs with Army security cooperation programs
Country team	Functional working groups for key areas		Better cross-training between services and agencies	TTPs for close cooperation with country team staff

CHAPTER FOUR

Option B: Increase Flexibility

Option B, "Increase Flexibility," has to do with long-term legislative and funding changes that are needed to increase the SAO's flexibility in security cooperation. This is essentially a question of spending authorities and the availability of funds. In particular, the ability to conduct certain types of training (on lethal and nonlethal techniques) or provide equipment to a host nation military is really about the authority to spend money on these tasks and the availability of funds for doing so. The RAND team sees two main challenges: (1) increasing the flexibility of existing funding sources and (2) providing new funding options that would increase flexibility.

Current Authorities

The authorities that govern security assistance and security cooperation are extremely complicated and frustrating to implement. As part of several other ongoing and recently completed studies, RAND has collected information on security cooperation programs from the Army, Air Force, and other U.S. government agencies and has attempted to decipher their authorities and programmatic restrictions, level of funding, and the main objectives of the programs (see Appendix B for an overview of Army security assistance and security cooperation programs and authorities).

This complicated set of authorities is not entirely accidental. In some cases, they address the intent of Congress. Typically, this challenge arises when a SAO wants to provide a host nation with the assistance that the security assistance officer feels is needed for a particular set of requirements based on an assessment of the situation in that country.

However, Congress has intentionally restricted the use of foreign assistance funds in order to maintain its oversight of the Executive Branch. For example, Congress wrote restrictions into the Foreign Assistance Act (FAA) that forbid the U.S. government from training, advising, or otherwise assisting foreign police forces except in specific circumstances as enumerated in the act.[1] The recommendations that follow are limited to those that could be implemented without requiring a fundamental change in the intent of Congress.

As noted in Chapter Two, the two major categories of authorities are Title 10 and Title 22 funding. Title 10 funding is more flexible in how it is used but has restrictions on what it may be used for. Specifically, at least 50 percent of the Title 10 funding must benefit U.S. military forces. Title 22 funding has no such national or agency restrictions, but it is authorized and

---

[1] See Foreign Assistance Act of 1986, P.L. 99-529, Section 660.

appropriated by program and often by country. This could be interpreted as limiting flexibility in how it is used as well as what it may be used for, though not in the same sense as Title 10 funds.

The existing restrictions fall into nested categories of programs and activities. We consider five major categories, presented below in increasing levels of required authorities and decreasing degrees of flexibility.

Programs That Provide Advice or Assistance but Do Not Provide Training or Equipment

Some examples of these types of programs are the Army Staff Talks program, Military Personnel Exchange Program (MPEP), Civil-Military Emergency Planning, the National Guard State Partnership Program (NGB-SPP), the Regional Centers, and the LOGEX logistics exercise. These programs, and others like them, form the bedrock of security cooperation and help to lay the groundwork for building relationships with allies and other partners. In addition to the Army, the Navy and Air Force have similar programs, as do a host of other U.S. government agencies, international organizations, and U.S. allies. Many of these services programs are paid for with Title 10 funds, which means that at least 50 percent of the benefits of these programs must accrue to the United States. However, this also implies that they cannot be used for SC/TAA[2] missions that primarily benefit a foreign military force.

Programs That Provide Training on Nonlethal Techniques to Foreign Militaries

These are generally funded through Title 22 (e.g., the IMET program, which brings foreign military officers to U.S. schools), although some programs are funded by Title 10 (e.g., the Western Hemisphere Institute for Security Cooperation).

This is potentially important in security sector reform as well, as many of these officers move up in their respective militaries to positions of power. The Global Peacekeeping Operations Initiative (GPOI) also falls within this category. GPOI is a new funding source for peacekeeping training. Its goal is to increase the supply of peacekeepers that are available for United Nations missions. GPOI funds can be used to train peacekeepers but cannot be used to equip them, a good example of the restrictions sometimes placed on programs.

Programs That Supply Equipment or Improve Infrastructure

The principal authority for these programs is Title 22, but DoD seems inclined to increase the size and reach of "1206 authority" (Section 1206 of the 2006 and 2007 National Defense Authorization Acts), which permits DoD to perform a broad range of security cooperation tasks to build partner military capacity in support of U.S. counterterrorism and combat operations.[3] Although this authority permits DoD to conduct a wide range of activities, including some that would normally fall under Title 22 authorities, it is restricted in how it can be used. For example, it cannot be used to enhance partner capacity in nonmilitary elements of security forces. The 1206 authority has been used for train and equip programs in Lebanon, Pakistan, and the Philippines.

---

[2] Although we give no formal definition of TAA missions, it is clear that they overlap significantly with security cooperation, but are not synonymous with it. For example, many security cooperation programs include no training, advising, or assisting (e.g., IMET, FMF) and TAA efforts can also include active assistance in combat operations. We use "SC/TAA "to indicate the programs that fall within the scope of this project, as defined in this chapter.

[3] National Defense Authorization Act of 2007, P.L. 109-163, Section 1206.

Programs That Provide Training on Lethal Techniques

There are only a handful of these programs. An important authority that permits training on lethal techniques is 1206 authority, which allows DoD to purchase equipment, deliver it, and train foreign nationals to use it—all using Title 10 funds. However, Congress has been reluctant to grant DoD multiyear authorization for 1206, arguing that it is the role of the State Department to provide this type of assistance. These programs are precisely the type needed to provide flexibility in non-peacetime environments because they are useful tools that bridge the gap between the slow-moving "peacetime" Title 22 security assistance system and the more immediate needs of key partners fighting terrorism and instability.[4]

Comprehensive Efforts to Train and Equip Foreign Security Forces

Examples are those efforts undertaken in Iraq and Afghanistan. These efforts are of a large scale, with special funding and authorities. Major efforts are often undertaken using a collection of programs that fall into more than one of the categories above. For example, the broad category of security force training, "Train and Equip Programs" (TEPs), is usually accomplished through programs and funding authorities that are cobbled together by various organizations. The Georgia Train and Equip Program mentioned in Chapter Three and discussed in greater depth in Appendix A is an example. Another in which agencies worked well together was the Trans Sahel Counter Terrorist Program, of which Operation Enduring Freedom–Trans Sahel was the military operational component. This program was created by a presidential directive and funded by a supplemental appropriation. It brought together several programs and agencies to provide counterterrorism training and equipment to several governments in the Sahel region of North Africa.[5]

Finally, the level of "normal" security cooperation diminishes rapidly as U.S. forces are deployed to actively engage in such operations as in Iraq and Afghanistan. At this point, the country team, and therefore the SAO, often ceases to be the driver of SC/TAA within the host nation and a Joint Task Force takes charge of security force assistance and training.[6] This is the point at which SC/TAA passes out of the scope of this study, so we do not pursue it further. However, we note that this is a critical transition and an area in which future research should be considered.

DoD rarely provides assistance for security forces other than the military, and the U.S. Army usually is not required to provide advisors to ministries—defense or other. However, the Army would—and does—provide support under extreme circumstances such as those presented recently in Iraq and Afghanistan. Specifically, the Army plans to provide tactical advisors, combat advisors, and service advisors to foreign armies, but not ministry advisors and not support to police, intelligence services, or other security agencies.[7]

---

[4] The efficacy of 1206 authority has not been studied. Before recommending that it be made permanent, such a study would be an important step.

[5] The Trans Sahel Counterterrorism Partnership included close coordination between DoD (OSD and the U.S. European Command) and the State Department on the planning and implementation of various activities within the program.

[6] Theoretically, the ambassador, as the President's representative to the host nation, should have cognizance over all efforts that affect U.S.–host nation relations, even when a large JTF is in country. In practice, this is often not the case.

[7] Brigadier General Edward P. Donnelly, Deputy Director, G-35, Headquarters, Department of the Army, unpublished briefing, "Army Approach to Security Force Assistance," September 2, 2009, Slide 4.

The Effect of Restrictions on Authorities

Restrictions on authorities associated with programs can affect U.S. efforts to work with partner countries in a variety of capacities, including SC/TAA. Figure 4.1 shows that a program's authorities can affect several variables. These variables, depicted along the y-axis, capture

- the programs available for specific types of partner capacity-building activities, including SC/TAA
- the U.S. capacity to conduct SC/TAA
- the ability of non-DoD agencies to contribute to SC/TAA.

The authorities for engaging partner countries in specific ways become more restrictive as one moves to the right on the x-axis. For example, the highest level of authority category is "Broader security force training," which is essentially training nonmilitary security forces. This course of action requires a presidential waiver. Building partner capacity activities in Iraq and Afghanistan is a good example. Training on lethal techniques also requires special permissions. Those programs are mostly found in the Special Forces community.

A few programs allow for training on nonlethal techniques and the provision of equipment, such as Title 22 security assistance (e.g., IMET), the Section 1206 (Title 10) train-and-equip programs, and the Title 10 counterterrorism fellowship program. In most of these programs, the Army controls the resources but does not decide the overall objectives for the program or the specific activities.

Figure 4.1
SC/TAA Categories and Authorities

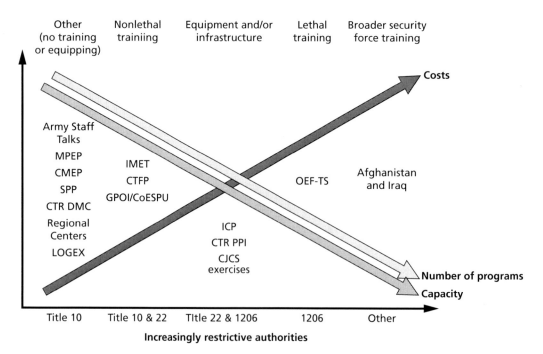

NOTE: Detail and references on the programs in this figure are in Appendix B. See the Abbreviations for full definitions.
RAND TR734-2.1

However, when we look outside of DoD to other interagency partners, such at the State Department, the Department of Homeland Security, and the Department of Energy, the capacity to work with nonmilitary security forces increases significantly. Such interagency programs include the Export Control and Related Border Security program, the Anti-Terrorism Assistance program, and GPOI, to name a few.

Broadly speaking, the Army has the most programs at its disposal in the first (nontraining/ other) category, where it controls the resources and decides the overall objectives. Some examples include Army-to-Army Staff Talks, the Military Personnel Exchange Program (MPEP), and the Civil-Military Emergency Preparedness (CMEP) program. However, there are several programs listed under this category where the Army manages the resources (i.e., money and manpower), but does not decide the overall objectives of the programs. A good example of this is the Chairman of the Joint Chiefs of Staff Exercises, where the ASCCs control the resources but the Joint Staff sets the broad objectives.

DoD's capacity to conduct the nontraining/other category of activities is also much greater than its capacity to engage partners in activities in the other four categories. For example, training nonmilitary security forces requires partnering with other interagency actors. In addition, it costs DoD much less to execute activities in the nontraining/other category than those activities found in the other four categories of authorities. Figure 4.1 illustrates how cost increase for programs further to the right on the x-axis. While not a hard-and-fast rule, this is generally the case.

Finally, if the Army would like to increase its ability to provide partners with training more fully across the spectrum of possible needs and operations, Congress would have to expand the authorities.

Authorities to Increase Flexibility

We next turn to what can be done to increase flexibility. The tangle of authorities is manageable within the current system during peaceful, nonemergency situations (as mentioned in Chapter Two), but is not sufficient for situations in which there is a need to respond quickly to unplanned events. Because this systemic inflexibility is rooted in law, any fundamental changes would require Congress to act.[8] However, Congress has provided additional flexibility to address complex emergencies through 1206 authority—a useful innovation. This authority permits DoD (with Department of State concurrence) to spend up to $300 million annually to build partner counterterror capabilities, as well as partner capabilities to be used in conflicts in which U.S. forces are engaged (excluding Iraq and Afghanistan).[9]

However, recent Congressional decisions denying DoD 1206 authority in Panama, for example, mean that this authority is limited for the purposes of this analysis. That is, it can be used for certain types of unplanned or dynamic events, as noted above, but it does not provide additional flexibility in other circumstances. Additionally, 1206 authority can be used only

[8]   Section 1206 (f) requires the President to provide a report to Congress on changes that would be required to the Foreign Assistant Act (and other laws) to increase the U.S. government's ability to build partner capacity, as well as needed changes to funding mechanisms and government organizations.

[9]   National Defense Authorization Act of 2007, Section 1206.

when U.S. forces are engaged in operations, a set of circumstances that will often fall outside of the scope of this study. Finally, 1206 authority is not permanent.

The discussion above points to a gap in authorities—one that will become larger if 1206 authority is not made permanent. We have stated that the following:

- Under peacetime circumstances, the current, permanent authorities could be sufficient, particularly if the changes recommended under Option A are adopted.
- Under other circumstances short of a deployed JTF, 1206 authority permits the training of counterterrorism forces.
- Under other circumstances that do not involve terrorism but that impact U.S. interests, there are no authorities that permit the flexible provision of security assistance or cooperation. This is a potentially significant gap.

Recommendations to Address the Gap in Authorities

To address this, the RAND team considered an additional authority designed to provide greater flexibility and quicker response times at the beginning of an effort. The Georgia Train and Equip Program is an example where this could have been useful. Because of its high priority, GTEP pooled together 16 funding sources from across the U.S. government—something that would have been difficult to achieve without presidential interest. The program had a relatively slow start, partly because it was so piecemeal. Further, coordination and deconfliction of the multitude of programs and the specific authorities attached to each program proved problematic later the in process. The concept presented here is modeled after the Stafford Act, which provides spending authorities and funding in case of domestic emergencies, such as natural disasters. The Stafford Act allows the President to declare an emergency and provides funds and spending authority for well-defined programs to specific agencies once the emergency is declared. This permits the federal government to respond quickly to a disaster.[10] It outlines conditions under which the Stafford Act can be invoked and requires notification to Congress. It also stipulates specific programs on which Stafford Act funds can be spent (e.g., repair, restoration, and replacement of damaged facilities; debris removal; federal assistance to individuals and households).

Similar legislation could be crafted for emergency circumstances in the national security arena that require prompt, flexible U.S. response in the form of SC/TAA missions with acceptable partners (e.g., as defined by the 1206 authority). Criteria for what constitutes an actionable emergency, as well as program categories (e.g., those in the Stafford Act), should be carefully defined by Congress to control what programs are permitted and under what conditions.

The key challenges outlined above would include authority

- for the ambassador to move funds from one program category to another—particularly important for Title 22 programs[11]
- to conduct training on nonlethal techniques
- to provide equipment and supplies

---

[10]   Robert T. Stafford Disaster Relief and Emergency Assistance Act, 1988.

[11]   Note that this authority is similar to the authorities given by the Support for Eastern European Democracies (SEED) Act of 1989 (P.L. 101-179) and the Freedom Support Act of 1992 (P.L. 102-511) to a designated Washington-based coordinator. This is not a new concept, and it could be adapted to security assistance.

- to conduct training on lethal techniques
- to conduct broader security force training and provide advice and assistance.

To be viable, the statute would need well-defined conditions under which the President might declare a need for each category of authorities, as well as prompt reporting requirements to Congress. The advantage of a mechanism similar to the Stafford Act is that it is a model with which Congress is familiar and comfortable. Should Congress want to make 1206 authority permanent, it could do so in this legislation.

Should no such legislation be forthcoming, DoD should consider two additional actions. The first is to draft model legislation for each of the authority categories discussed above. This model legislation, if shared with Congress ahead of time, could be ready for adoption upon need, thus cutting down on the amount of time needed to draft, discuss, and pass good legislation in an emergency.[12] A last option would be to examine the inherent powers of the President to delineate what he or she can do without Congress in situations in which U.S. national security is threatened by actions abroad. If these were powers were deemed sufficiently broad, DoD could draft stand-by executive orders by which the President would activate and delegate these powers in times of need.[13] It is worth noting that the circumstances in which such an extraordinary measure may be needed would be few, and in those few cases, authority from Congress would likely be forthcoming. Nonetheless, it is an option that could be explored. We call these last two options (draft legislation and executive orders) "pocket authorities" for brevity's sake.

Implications for Option B: Increase Flexibility

The goal of Option B is to increase the flexibility of the SAO to perform its functions through examining and making recommendations for changes to the legal authorities that govern the execution of SC/TAA efforts. However, in doing so, we cannot simply rewrite the body of statutes on security cooperation because they reflect the intent of Congress. Thus, Option B has limited but potentially profound implications.

This option implies a need to propose legislation, including the need to explore the possibility of "pocket authorities" in particular. This, in turn, implies coordinating with the Congress and doing the legal research necessary to determine what pocket executive orders are possible. The Army's role in these efforts would be limited to supporting OSD.

The implications of this option are summarized in Table 4.1, below, which carries forward the format used in Table 3.1. In addition, the RAND research team believes that an analysis of the benefits from 1206 authority should be undertaken to see whether it should be made permanent. The Army may want to take the initiative to do this on its own.

---

[12] The State Department's Coordinator for Reconstruction and Stability (S/CRS) has developed a "Unified Action Plan" that attempts to outline some of the mechanisms needed for the U.S. government to respond to such crises. However, the plan is not yet operational and it is unclear whether it will be implemented.

[13] There is precedent for such standby executive orders in classified programs dealing with threats to the United States at home.

Table 4.1
Implications of Option B: Increase Flexibility

Level	Organization	Manpower	Training	Doctrine
Washington, D.C.	Propose authorities changes			Explore "pocket" authorities options
Army	Support authorities changes Study 1206 effectiveness			

Summary

In summary, this option builds on Option A and recommends three principal new authorities, funding mechanisms, or actions that could be taken to more rapidly implement changes to authorities when needed. These suggestions have the merit of having a precedent in other aspects of law and practice—albeit in other types of emergencies. These recommendations are as follows:

- Fill the gap left by 1206 authority through Stafford Act–like legislation and funding mechanisms (into which 1206 authority could be incorporated if deemed advisable). Doing so would permit additional flexibility and funding upon presidential declaration while carefully stipulating the conditions under which such declarations could be made, the programs under which funds could be spent, and the requirements for reporting to Congress.
- Prepare "pocket" legislation to be presented to the Congress that would provide the flexibility and funding needed under anticipatable conditions of need.
- Prepare "pocket "executive orders for presidential signature that would provide the additional authorities under anticipatable conditions of need.

CHAPTER FIVE

Option C: Shape and Assist

In this chapter, we present an option for the organization and approach of the SAO that would help in the train, advise, and assist mission. The option could stand alone but would be most effective if it builds on or is executed in conjunction with Option A, which seeks to improve the operation of SAOs by formalizing cooperation and coordination measures to make the most of the current structure and authorities, and with Option B, which improves the suite of security assistance and cooperation authorities to provide the SAO with greater flexibility, capacity, and capabilities. Option C would give the SDO additional authority over all SC/TAA efforts operating in country, and additional, different staff to manage this quasi-operational effort, such as in FID. Although Option C would not be appropriate for every country, it could be a critical element in U.S. national security efforts for countries of high importance facing significant threats.

Under this option, the SDO would be responsible for and direct most military personnel in country—except for those conducting military operations under RCC command—using a staff that would be capable of managing a full TAA effort. Because the SDO works for the Chief of Mission, putting him or her in charge of these activities would make the Chief of Mission responsible for all activities that do not fall explicitly under a combatant commander. Giving the SDO this responsibility would require more than the six personnel currently authorized by statute for the SAO. Currently, a handful of embassies have large in-country contingents (e.g., Colombia has over 100 military personnel and other countries, such as Egypt and the Philippines, have smaller contingents that exceed the statutory six).

The SDO would also have the ability to request, accept, and manage out-of-country assets. This could include requesting units from the Army Force Generation process, Military Training Teams (MTTs), assets from U.S. Army Training and Doctrine Command such as SATMO teams, or other structures are currently being considered (e.g., other service capabilities). Special operations forces (SOF) and intelligence agencies conducting "black" operations may fall into a different category; it is currently unclear how an embassy-led SC/TAA effort would coordinate with SOF conducting operations under Global War on Terrorism auspices, or if they would at all. However, SOF personnel at the embassy would take direction from the SDO on white operations, and he or she would be fully cognizant of their other efforts. As a minimum, the SDO should be able to coordinate military interagency involvement and assets in security cooperation efforts for the U.S. ambassador. The SDO should also have the ability to hand off SC/TAA efforts to a larger military operational effort if the situation dictates.

Option C also requires military personnel with the ability to act with great political sensitivity and with a good understanding of U.S. foreign policy goals in their country and how military efforts fit within this framework—in particular, the execution of advisory and assistance missions. In this regard, political efforts will all but certainly be needed to ensure that military efforts fit within this larger context and contribute to these larger goals. These missions also require close coordination with the embassy political staff, the INL, the Department of Justice representative at the embassy (if present), the legal attaché, and USAID, as a minimum. That said, not every partner facing an insurgency will need the same kind of U.S. military support.

To develop this option, we extract lessons from several current and historical counterinsurgency (COIN) and FID cases for SDO authority—as well as SAO organization, mission, training, experience, and civil-military coordination—that might be applied to future situations in which the U.S. government is supporting a partner country's counterinsurgency efforts. Although we use these lessons to develop some broad implications for the U.S. military if it were to pursue a full-fledged TAA capability, we also suggest a range of potential SAO requirements that depend on the level of partner political-military difficulty and the extent of U.S. military intervention in the host country.

Unity of Effort for TAA Endeavors

Currently, no individual DoD official controls all military elements involved in security cooperation activities in most countries. Authority varies depending on the country, the function that is being performed, and the organization that is performing it. For example, in Colombia, SOF are under the tactical control of the SAO (called the military group [MILGP] in Colombia) for force protection. Although the SAO designs their in-country requirements, SOF are otherwise controlled by other organizations. Also, the SAO in Colombia provides support to a host of DoD and non-DoD players involved in law enforcement, counterinsurgency, and counterdrug efforts. The multitude of agencies in country and the lack of clear lines of authority foster bureaucratic stovepiping. As resources became more constrained, the security assistance officer in Colombia recognized that DoD's various pieces (at least) had to be better integrated. Consequently, he implemented a "supported/supporting" command concept with other defense entities in country, with himself as the supported military "commander."[1] In his view, this in-country clarification of authorities and relationships has improved the efficiency of SC/TAA operations, even though he does not directly control all DoD elements in country and these relationships are based on informal agreements. This officer asserted that these ad hoc supporting/supported relationships need to be embedded in an operations order or a deployment order to improve performance of DoD assets deploying into the country. This is particularly important in the case of military intelligence operators and SOF. Better yet, following the recommendation to institutionalize "best practices" espoused in Option A, this relationship could be written into DoD policy guidance as well as into appropriate orders. The goal would be to make the SAO semioperational while respecting the equities of the variety of DoD organizations operating in a country such as Colombia.[2]

---

[1] As will become evident in the discussion that follows, the SAO does not command the TAA assets in theater. The Colombia effort is a great example of how efficiency can be significantly improved by creative efforts to improve coordination and cooperation, as shown in Option A.

[2] Interview with COL Kevin D. Saderup, current MILGROUP Commander in Colombia, May 2008.

As stated in Chapter Three, the division of responsibility between the SAO and DAO in security assistance/cooperation has been a problem in some embassies. In Georgia and Armenia, the DAO has oversight of exercises, and implementation of programs such as participation in the George C. Marshall European Center for Security Studies and the Warsaw Initiative Fund. The SAO (called the Office of Defense Cooperation—ODC—in these countries) is responsible for security assistance and the Counter-Terrorism Fellowship Program (CTFP). But the SAO would normally have responsibility for all Title 22 and Title 10 security cooperation activities. For example, exercises currently under DAO purview could be used to validate the training provided by FMF and IMET funding managed by the SAO. In Colombia, the relationship between the SAO and the DAO has also at times been problematic. Although personal relationships have mitigated conflicts in the past, "the system is built for friction," especially when the defense attaché (DATT) and the SAO are senior officers of equivalent rank. The SAO represents the U.S. Southern Command commander, who has a major interest in building partner capabilities and controls the majority of DoD resources in country. The defense attaché reports to DIA and is largely separated from the security cooperation effort but is designated the senior officer.[3]

It is unclear whether the new SDO policy will provide greater SC/TAA unity of effort or resolve the SAO-DAO dilemma. The policy has not yet been widely implemented and there are ongoing debates over who will be the SDO in particular countries.[4] According to DoD Directive 5105.75, the new SDO will have coordinating but not command authority over all DoD elements assigned or attached to, or operating from, U.S. embassies. Specifically, the SDO will

- serve as defense attaché and chief of security assistance
- act as the in-country focal point for planning, coordinating, supporting, and/or executing U.S. defense issues and activities in the host nation, including Theater Security Cooperation programs
- present coordinated DoD views on all defense matters to the Chief of Mission (COM) and act as the single DoD point of contact to the COM to assist in carrying out his or her responsibilities.

Importantly, the SDO's coordinating authority over DoD elements will "not preempt the authority exercised over these elements by the COM, the mission authority exercised by the parent DoD components, or the command authority exercised by the RCC." Additionally, the SDO will not have the authority to impose punishment under the Uniform Code of Military Justice.[5]

---

[3] Interview with COL Saderup, 2008.

[4] These debates may be having a negative impact on SCO operations. According to one commander, the SDO policy has not been well planned or coordinated. Although he supports the concept of a single DoD official in the embassy who has overall authority, he argues that it is very important in some countries that the transition to a new authority structure be handled with care, and that the person who is selected for the job have the right kind and level of experience.

[5] DoD Directive 5105.75, 2007.

Increased Capacity to Manage Military Aspects of SC/TAA

In previous FID efforts, limits on U.S. military manpower in country have created difficulties for the provision of SC/TAA, causing the U.S. government to rely on militarily inappropriate or legally questionable training and advisory means. For example, in March 1981, Congress capped the SAO in El Salvador at 55 "trainers." Since it was estimated that a cadre of 50 to 60 was the minimum required in country, other options were tried for training Salvadoran Army battalions. The SAO developed a plan to train an immediate reaction battalion at Fort Bragg whose cost was equivalent to training six to eight battalions in El Salvador.[6] In addition, U.S. political authorities found it expedient to fudge on the 55-man ceiling. As a result, the number of U.S. military personnel in El Salvador grew to over 100.[7]

It is important to keep in mind that constraints on U.S. military manpower involved in TAA do not necessarily result in bad outcomes. The ceiling on the number of U.S. military personnel in El Salvador forced the Salvadorans to prioritize their requirements and enabled the SAO to modify its requirements list based on the availability of American trainers. Most important, the 55-man limit helped keep the war an essentially Salvadoran effort, which limited the level of opposition in Washington to the FID effort.[8] As U.S. officials focusing on Central America in the 1980s were keenly aware, large numbers of U.S. advisors and support personnel had not led to a reduction in the strength of the insurgency in Vietnam in the 1950s and 1960s. By the end of 1968, the Military Advisory Assistance Group, Vietnam (MAAG-V) had reached 11,596 personnel—the equivalent of seven U.S. Army divisions in terms of officers and senior noncommissioned officers (NCOs). According to John Nagl, "The huge size and unwieldy structure of the Military Assistance Command Vietnam made not only change but also learning extremely difficult."[9]

In 2004, Congress acceded to 'DoD's wish for more flexibility regarding the number of U.S. military training and advisory personnel permitted to assist the government of Colombia in its counternarcotics and counterinsurgency efforts. But the number of U.S. personnel in Colombia in the last several years has never come close to the limit.[10] What distinguishes the Colombia SAO from other security cooperation organizations is less its size than the way it is structured. During the past three years, the SAO has been transformed from a standard security assistance organization to an operational organization focused on security cooperation that is embedded in the country team and responsible to both the combatant commander and the ambassador. Tailored to its unique mission, there is no other SAO in the Southern Command area of operations quite like Colombia's. On the one hand, the SAO supports the current

---

[6]   Robert D. Ramsey III, *Advising Indigenous Forces: American Advisors in Korea, Vietnam, and El Salvador*, Global War on Terrorism Occasional Paper 18, Fort Leavenworth, Kansas: Combat Studies Institute Press, 2006, p. 84.

[7]   Tommie Sue Montgomery, "Fighting Guerrillas: The United States and Low-Intensity Conflict in El Salvador," *New Political Science*, Vol. 9, No. 18–19, Autumn 1990, p. 35.

[8]   John D. Waghelstein, "Ruminations of a Pachyderm or What I Learned in the Counter-insurgency Business," *Small Wars and Insurgencies*, Vol. 5, No. 3, Winter 1994, p. 365.

[9]   John A. Nagl, *Learning to Eat Soup with a Knife*, Chicago & London: University of Chicago Press, 2002, p. 180.

[10]   Andrew Feickert, *U.S. Military Operations in the Global War on Terrorism: Afghanistan, Africa, the Philippines, and Colombia*, Washington, D.C.: Congressional Research Service, February 4, 2005, pp. 13–14.

campaign plan while refraining from engagement in combat operations. On the other hand, it is also focused on the long-term objective of establishing Colombia as a regional partner.[11]

Implications for the Army

In addition to these requirements for the SAO as part of the country team, expanding the responsibility of the SDO and his staff has implications for the Army. In particular, there will be more demanding requirements on SAO staffs to manage and direct a host of operations ongoing in the host country, and the likely requirement for more capacity than currently exists in Army security assistance/security cooperation organizations such as SATMO and Army Special Forces Command (see Table 5.1).

Expanded Mission for SAO

In previous FID situations, the U.S. military's mission in a partner country has generally gone beyond the provision of training and equipment. During the Vietnam War, the U.S. advisory role expanded over a ten-year period. For example, MAAG-V officials—first assigned to the regiment for infantry units and to the battalion for artillery, armor, and Marine Corps units—were later permitted to accompany South Vietnamese battalion and company units in combat to observe and offer advice.[12] In El Salvador in the 1980s, the principal SAO goal was the "professionalization" of the Salvadoran military.[13] El Salvador's National Campaign Plan developed by the SAO and other members of the country team in late 1982 was "a comprehensive, integrated political-economic-military plan that involved the armed forces, several government ministries including agriculture, economy, health and education, and the civilian population in the countryside."[14]

In response to the War on Terror, the U.S. military's role in Colombia shifted from supporting the war against drugs to a much wider counterinsurgency mission. In its 2003 budget

Table 5.1
Implications for the Army of Added Responsibilities

Responsibility	Army Implications
Expanded mission for SAO	Develop doctrine and increase available personnel
Ensure personnel with relevant experience and skills are available	Establish recruiting, training, retention, and leader development programs
Provide SC/TAA capacity beyond those in current assets	Modified force mix, including use of general purpose forces, as trainers/advisors

---

[11] Interview with COL Saderup.

[12] Ramsey, pp. 28–31.

[13] Ramsey, p. 86.

[14] Montgomery, pp. 35–38. Note, however, that this is the view of the SAO. A senior foreign service officer interviewed for this project who served in El Salvador during this time period recalled that the SAO responded to the U.S. Southern Command commander, not to the ambassador, and did not feel the SAO was a well integrated member of the country team.

proposal, the Bush administration requested approximately $100 million to train and equip two new Colombian army brigades to protect the Cano Limon–Covenas oil pipeline[15] and to create a Colombian Special Forces commando battalion to capture or kill guerrilla and paramilitary leaders, among other things.[16]

Relevant Experience and Skills for SAO Personnel

Historically, the U.S. military has not done a good job of preparing its forces to undertake large-scale SC/TAA missions. According to one former senior Vietnam advisor, the advisory role was "entirely new and challenging to most American soldiers [who] spent most of their lives giving and executing orders."[17] In the 1950s, no particular selection criteria were required for military advisors except rank, military occupation specialty, and availability for an overseas tour.[18] In the early 1960s, the U.S. Army's personnel system could not provide the large number of experienced advisors that was being demanded."[19] Standards for provincial and district advisors increased in late 1960s, but it was still hard to find qualified people who would take the job.[20] Americans and South Vietnamese lived in two different worlds, separated by a "linguistic and cultural barrier . . . that was almost impossible for the advisor to breach." This fact remained despite advisor training programs.[21]

Although a much smaller effort, the El Salvador advisory program, like its Vietnam predecessor, suffered from lack of well-qualified personnel and inadequate preparation and training.[22] Although personnel with a Special Forces background and Spanish-language capability were sought by the SAO, no formal training was provided before their arrival in El Salvador other than a 2.5-day general, non–El Salvador-specific Security Assistance Team Training and Orientation Course.[23]

One observation from these and other case studies is clear: Without an institutional capability to prepare military personnel for SC/TAA missions, they will—at least at the onset of an effort—not have the requisite skills needed for success. As the U.S. government faces expanding SC/TAA requirements, the need for more advisory training for conventional forces becomes clearer. According to the Colombia SAO, "SOF grow up doing that [training and advising foreign militaries]. General Purpose forces (GPF) are not used to operating individu-

---

[15] Andrew B. Tickner, "Colombia and the United States: From Counternarcotics to Counterterrorism," *Current History*, February 2003, p. 81.

[16] Adam Isacson, "Optimism, Pessimism, and Terrorism: The United States and Colombia in 2003," *Brown Journal of World Affairs,* Vol. 10, No. 2, Spring 2004, p. 247.

[17] Ramsey, p. 34–35.

[18] Ramsey, p. 37.

[19] Ramsey, p. 33.

[20] Ramsey, p. 39.

[21] Ramsey, p. 44.

[22] Ramsey, pp. 88–89.

[23] Ramsey, p. 91.

ally. They don't understand that one screw-up could have strategic consequences. They don't operate in three-man teams embedded with allies, dealing with other agencies."[24]

TAA Capacity Beyond Initial Assets

The historical tendency in FID situations has been for U.S. military SC/TAA capacity to increase beyond the initial assets located in the capital region. In Vietnam, the advisory effort moved to lower and lower levels of the host nation military and the provincial administration in response to the deteriorating situation in South Vietnam.[25] As in Vietnam (albeit on a much smaller scale), the U.S. advisory effort in El Salvador moved from the embassy into the field in the form of brigade advisors and combat support providers.[26] Currently, the SAO in Colombia directs an advisory effort built around Planning and Assistance Training Teams that are embedded with key Colombian operational units. These teams are augmented with Military Training Teams (MTTs) that satisfy niche requirements (e.g., close air support and intelligence). Personnel requirements for Planning and Assistance Training Teams and MTTs are filled through two different processes. The Army works through the Security Assistance Training Management Organization (SATMO) at Ft. Bragg, whereas the Marine Corps and Air Force rely on individual augmentees. These two processes are funded separately and difficult to orchestrate in country. According to the Colombia SAO, the services should pay more attention to personnel administration to support DoD's security cooperation mission. For example, the current system is set up to provide short-term temporary duty (TDY) personnel, yet "temporary duty" of four months to a year is the norm in Colombia. As a result, some individuals arrive administratively unprepared for an extended stay in country.[27]

Additional SAO Characteristics

In addition to the capabilities listed above, some characteristics of SAOs could be desirable in certain circumstances arising as part of a challenging TAA effort. Note that these characteristics would depend on the situation in which the effort was being conducted. In particular, they might be important in demanding FID circumstances in which soldiers (and civilians) would be on unaccompanied tours of duty, and in which the success of the overall effort relies on the combined effects of security assistance/security cooperation and other aspects of foreign assistance, such as Economic Support Funds programs and humanitarian assistance efforts. In particular, the SAO might want to

- have personnel remain for longer than one year in hardship posts because building and maintaining relationships with host nation officials is even more critical during dangerous times than during peacetime
- foster unity of effort between the military and civilian components of assistance efforts.

---

[24] Interview with COL Saderup.

[25] Dale Andrade, and LCOL James H. Willbanks, "CORDS/Phoenix: Counterinsurgency Lessons from Vietnam for the Future," *Military Review*, March–April 2006, p. 16.

[26] Ramsey, p. 89.

[27] Interview with COL Saderup.

With respect to this last characteristic, we continue to assume a situation in which U.S. forces are not operating in a direct combat role or conducting operations under the direction of a combatant commander (e.g., there is no JTF in country), and so the Chief of Mission continues to be responsible for all aspects of assistance to the host nation. As such, although unity of effort within the country team might exist in theory, during stressful situations, the ambassador has little time to ensure that unity of effort. Thus, unity of effort works best if it can be developed below the level of ambassador. Consideration of organizational structures that ensure unity of effort between the SAO and other members of the country team will be critical.

Length of Tours

The U.S. military's traditional practice of one-year tours of duty for permanent-change-of-station personnel—and shorter tours for TDY personnel—in hardship posts has been problematic for SC/TAA efforts in FID situations. Officially, a one-year unaccompanied tour was the standard for advisors in Vietnam; however, most served only 11 months. "The short tour provided little incentive to tackle difficult cultural and language barriers, much less a long-term approach to improving the Republic of Vietnam Armed Forces (RVNAF)."[28] During the initial period of the war in El Salvador, many MTTs rotated into El Salvador on TDY and others served in Honduras for three- to six-month tours. Reportedly, U.S. Ambassador Thomas Pickering "had an enormous problem" with short tours for military personnel, lamenting that "we were constantly running people through there who had to relearn." A one-year tour was better than shorter tours, but it was not long enough since it took "three to six months for a new advisor to adequately familiarize himself with the enemy situation and the history of the conflict."[29]

Civil-Military Unity of Effort

The record of modern FID campaigns indicates that the importance of civil-military unity of effort increases largely in proportion to the depth of social disorder and insecurity in the partner nation. Whether this unity is achieved through greater civil or military authority and control seems not to matter as much as the fact that a single official should be placed in charge of government efforts to assist the host nation. For example, Great Britain's 1950s counterinsurgency in Malaya was hampered by disarray within the colonial administration until Gerald Templar was appointed High Commissioner of Malaya and Director of Operations in 1952.[30] According to John Nagl, overcoming organizational resistance to change in Malaya required

---

[28] Ramsey, pp. 38–39.

[29] Ambassador Pickering, as quoted in Max G. Manwaring and Court Prisk, eds., *El Salvador and War: An Oral History of Conflict from the 1979 Insurrection to the Present*, Washington, D.C.: National Defense University Press, 1988, pp. 243–244. Secondary quote in Ramsey, p. 90.

[30] Mark Henniker Bart, "The Emergency in Malaya, 1948–60," *Journal of the Royal Central Asian Society*, Vol. 51, No. 1, 1964, pp. 37–38.

. . . the dramatic intervention of a single man who held absolute civil and military power to defeat the insurgents and would use that power and his personality to ensure that everyone concerned with the emergency adopted and implemented the lessons learned at such cost during its worst years."[31]

A decade later, in nearby Vietnam, the loosely coordinated U.S. country team concept did not produce the unity of effort necessary to shore up a weak South Vietnamese government and military in the face of a formidable Viet Cong insurgency. By the mid-1960s, U.S. agencies in Vietnam began fielding their own structures for operations in the provinces, acting under wholly separate chains of command. President Johnson initially tried to unify the pacification effort by putting Ambassador Henry Cabot Lodge in charge of all efforts in Vietnam.[32] However, GEN William Westmoreland and National Security Council official Robert Komer argued that with 90 percent of the resources, it was "obvious" that only the military "had the clout" to get the job done. In April 1967, the creation of the Civil Operations and Revolutionary Development Support (CORDS) program "unambiguously placed the military in charge of pacification." Ambassador Komer took the post of Deputy Commander of Military Assistance Command, Vietnam (MACV) for CORDS. Below him, various other civilians and civilian agencies were integrated into the military hierarchy.[33] Although many civilian officials in Vietnam were initially skeptical of the new military-controlled pacification command, "subordinating civilian capabilities to the military chain of command actually realized the principle of the primacy of civil power" by giving civilians greater influence over the use of military resources than they ever had before.[34] Partly as a result, the U.S. government as a whole began to pay much more attention to pacification requirements. Focused on defeating the Viet Cong insurgency, however, "CORDS did not possess the personnel, organization, or structure to enhance the legitimacy and thus the popularity of the South Vietnamese government."[35]

Unlike in Vietnam, the allocation of full authority over all matters in country to the U.S. ambassador in Laos improved the efficiency, if not the effectiveness, of security assistance to the Laotian government during the 1960s and 1970s.[36] In effect, the war in Laos became "William Sullivan's war" (Sullivan was U.S. ambassador from December 1964 until March 1969).[37] On the one hand, this degree of control enabled the ambassador "to take definitive positions, to move on his own initiative, and to press the agency heads under him to move rapidly in

---

[31] Nagl, p. 81.

[32] Robert W. Komer, *Bureaucracy Does Its Thing: Institutional Constraints on U.S.-GVN Performance in Vietnam*, Santa Monica, Calif.: RAND Corporation, R-967-ARPA, 1972, pp. 84–85. President Johnson gave Ambassadors Lodge and Taylor full authority over MACV, but neither accepted it. At one point, it was even suggested that Gen. Westmoreland or another suitable person assume the role of Chief of Staff to the Ambassador. Furthermore, the Army's PROVN study recommended the Ambassador be designated the single person in charge of all efforts (p. 87). See also Andrade and Willbanks, 2006, pp.12–13.

[33] Andrade and Willbanks, 2006, pp. 13–14.

[34] MAJ Ross Coffey, "Revisiting CORDS: The Need for Unity of Effort to Secure Victory in Iraq," *Military Review*, March–April 2006, pp. 29–30.

[35] Coffey, p. 32.

[36] Simpson, Erin M., "The Country Team in Laos, 1965–1973," *The Country Team in American Strategy*, unpublished manuscript, December 2006, p. 7.

[37] Simpson, p. 9.

the desired direction."[38] On the other hand, "This pattern of close, occasionally, domineering, ambassadorial control . . . also complicated the military assistance program for Laos, whose procedures were already fairly convoluted" as a result of the restrictions on the U.S. military presence in Laos imposed by the Geneva Accords.[39]

The lesson to be taken is that, in very demanding circumstances, such as a robust U.S. FID effort (e.g., in Laos in the 1960s and 1970s and El Salvador in the 1980s), unity of effort may be needed beyond merely DoD programs and operations. In particular, efforts may extend beyond those of the military, making true unity of effort on the part of the entire country team important. This means that security cooperation organization (SCO) personnel assigned to these countries will need political-military skills that are at a higher level than those required in most situations and truly coordinated efforts with other agencies (e.g., USAID) and embassy sections (e.g., the Political, Economic, and Political-Military sections, INL representative) will pay large dividends.

Before leaving this topic, we note that we have not addressed the question of how to characterize those circumstances in which some or all of these capabilities would be needed. We outline important considerations below and provide more extensive notes in Appendix C.

- *Existence, size, and strength of an insurgency*
  - The effectiveness of SC/TAA will depend in large part on the existence, size, and strength of an insurgency in a partner country. For example, increased U.S. military assistance to the Salvadoran military in the 1980s could not eradicate the Farabundo Marti National Liberation Front (FMLN), although it probably prevented a rebel takeover in El Salvador. In Colombia, the government currently faces three different insurgencies that pose different threats; the Revolutionary Armed Forces of Colombia (FARC), in particular, is unlikely to give up easily despite recent Colombian military gains made possible by U.S. TAA programs.
- *Geography (size, borders, terrain, etc.) of the host nation*
  - Geography can contribute to the severity of a conflict and the skills needed to contain it. For example, countering the insurgencies in Colombia is made more challenging by its geography—large, complex terrain; lack of infrastructure in the countryside; and long borders with not-too-helpful neighbors.
- *Capabilities of the host nation*
  - Government competence and openness
    o Government competence and openness affect the likelihood of SC/TAA success. A centrist civilian government was a weak reed on which to pin U.S. hopes for reform in El Salvador when the anti-reform military held most of the power. Although Colombia's counterinsurgency prospects have begun to look brighter, its central government has historically been weak in terms of major government functions and a presence outside the larger cities.
  - Security host nation forces' size, quality, loyalty, and organizational culture
    o Host nation force size, quality, loyalty, and culture will play a major role in determining what SC/TAA programs, if any, a country will need and the level of suc-

---

[38] Simpson, p. 19.

[39] Simpson, p. 9.

cess they achieve. For example, the corruption and politicization of the Army of the Republic of Vietnam weighed heavily against U.S. TAA efforts in South Vietnam. Likewise, the Salvadoran Army's poor training and equipment, brutality, unpopularity, and resistance to institutional reform prolonged the conflict in El Salvador notwithstanding significant U.S. aid. Furthermore, some question whether U.S. SC/TAA can build the capacity of Colombia's military to the point where it will be able to defeat the various insurgencies it faces.

- *U.S. national interests and policies*
  - U.S. interests and policy provide the framework in which SC/TAA takes place. When these interest and policies are perceived to be in conflict with each other, they complicate DoD's job of providing delivering the appropriate kind of security assistance. For example, U.S. military attempts to increase the effectiveness of the El Salvadoran Armed Forces (ESAF) were affected by policymakers' varying emphases on U.S. strategic interests in Central America and their human rights policy in El Salvador. Furthermore, some argue that Congressional constraints on the provision of assistance to Colombia have hindered administration attempts to create a coherent TAA strategy.

For a more thorough discussion of the contextual factors affecting the provision of TAA, including historical references, see Appendix C.

The case studies discussed above are summarized in Table 5.2.

Figure 5.1 is a diagram of an enhanced SCO compatible with Option C, which is based on the current structure of the Colombia MILGP and the considerations discussed above.

Figure 5.1
Enhanced Security Cooperation Organization (Option C)

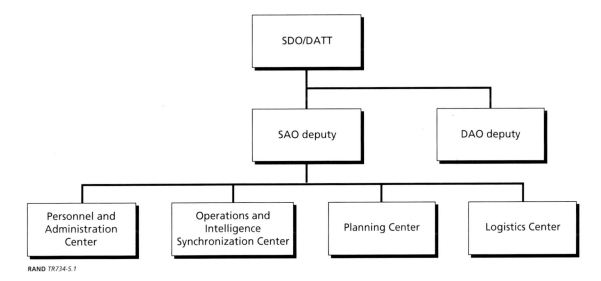

RAND *TR734-5.1*

Table 5.2
Case Studies from FID and COIN Operations

Type of Operation	Military Command	Manpower	Mission	Experience and Training	Civil-Military Coordination
Vietnam					
One large insurgency/ conventional threat COIN	MACV extended control over various pacification efforts with mixed results	Number of combat unit and territorial advisors reached almost 11,600 by 1969	Importance of TAA mission waxed and waned for 20 years	Incentives for experienced advisors did not work as expected Training improved over time, but never enough	Military-dominated civil-military advisory organization (CORDS)
El Salvador					
One small insurgency FID	MILGP controlled in-country "trainers"; control over Honduras-based forces unclear	Tight U.S. manpower limits circumvented, with mixed results	TAA goal of establishing professional Economic Support Funds difficult to achieve	Limited pool of qualified SOF supplemented with GPF Short Security Assistance course	Integrated country team in theory, but with considerable MILGP autonomy
Colombia					
Three insurgencies FID	MILGP established a supported/ supporting concept for forces not under its control	U.S. manpower ceiling raised and so far not reached	TAA implications of shift from CN to COIN not fully apparent	Lack of TAA training and doctrine for GPF dealt with through on-the-job training	Integrated embassy country team; considerable MILGP autonomy

Implications of Option C: Shape and Assist

The implications of this option are the most profound, although they are limited to a small number of countries. Additionally, because each country's circumstances will be different, the extent of the changes envisioned here may differ in each case. The major categories of changes could be summarized as the following:

- Importance of aligning SC/TAA efforts with overarching U.S. foreign policy goals. The very importance of these countries, which justifies Option C in the first place, indicates the need for a unified approach toward achieving U.S. foreign policy goals.
  - Conceptualizing these efforts in terms of political-military considerations becomes more important than in other countries; the skills needed to integrate military and civilian efforts in the security sector, as well as across the board, become more important.
  - The ability to establish and maintain good relations with the host nation is more important than in other countries.
  - Knowledge of the host nation's culture and language are important for SAOs to adequately train, assist, and advise countries confronting an insurgency. Such circumstances also require experienced personnel who remain in country for more than a few months at a time.

- Civilian agencies are not designed to address the civilian-oriented tasks required in insurgencies or other similar circumstances. DoD may need to loan personnel who can help civilian agencies in Washington and the field to properly man their operational efforts, with an eye on the issue of "over-militarizing" U.S. embassies.
  - If this concept is valid, there are implications for the SDO rating scheme. In particular, if the ambassador is truly to be in charge of the overall U.S. effort in country, the ambassador's principal subordinates should unambiguously work for him or her.
- Changes in authority of the SDO. The SDO should be able to oversee and manage all U.S. military efforts ongoing in country even if he/she does not directly control all advisory and training assistance elements (e.g., "black" SOF and intelligence teams).
  - The SDO should be accorded "command-like" authority over most permanent and temporary security assistance teams, including Uniform Code of Military Justice authority.
  - SDO duties should entail support for the current campaign plan (excluding combat activities) as well as long-term security cooperation and intelligence gathering.
- An enhanced SDO organization compatible with a TAA mission should be designed for coordination and synchronization. It should consist of an operational structure embedded in the embassy country team that reports to the regional combatant commander and the ambassador. The existing Colombia MILGP is a potential model with its "center" organization. Such an organization might consist of the following:
  - The SDO/defense attaché (DATT) as commander of SCO, responsible for long term planning of security cooperation and intelligence gathering activities and liaising with senior host nation and U.S. officials
  - A deputy responsible for the day-to-day operations of the SAO, including
    o an Operations and Intelligence Synchronization Center responsible for situational awareness, force protection, trends assessment, and distinguished visitors
    o a Planning Center that is structured to conduct and coordinate planning with all DoD and civilian agencies of interest
    o a Security Cooperation Logistics Center responsible for security assistance case and contract management, training funds, institutional reform, and logistical functions, and liaison activities
    o an Administration Center responsible for resource management and personnel administration
    o the ability to conduct "normal" SAO activities (e.g., FMF, foreign military sales [FMS], IMET).
  - A deputy responsible for day-to-day operations of the DAO, and the ability to conduct "normal" DAO activities.
- Changes in the composition and skills of the SAO staff make be called for to permit it to manage efforts that may at times be quasi-operational, including the following:
  - number of military personnel permitted in country
  - length of military personnel tours (longer than one year)
  - skill sets of staff, including cultural and language skills
  - ability to conduct a host of efforts ranging from assessments, requests for forces (RFF), and comprehensive management.
- Policies, doctrine, and TTPs will be needed at all levels to make this a relatively standard professional task in which personnel can be trained.

- Army personnel policy leaders should consider whether or not there is a requirement for a new skill identifier or occupational specialty for security cooperation personnel (SCP).

Option C is summarized in Table 5.3.

Table 5.3
Implications of Option C: Shape and Assist

Level	Organization	Manpower	Training	Doctrine
Washington, D.C.		Possible reinforcement of USAID, State, other government agencies DoD policy on loaned manpower to civilian agencies for security cooperation tasks		Political-military doctrine Presidential Decision Directive on regional interagency organizations
Army	Capability to Generate TAA assets Train soldiers in TAA tasks Collect and make available security cooperation lessons learned	Full spectrum of TAA Army and general skills Career field implications Numbers dependent on requirements	Political-military skill sets	Doctrine for managing TAA up to and including FID in counter terrorism or in conjunction with JTF
Region	Regional interagency organizations			
ASCC	Ability to coordinate and support SC/TAA assets in regional countries	Establish cadre of SC/TAA administrators	Improve political-military skills, language, and cultural awareness of SC/TAA personnel	TTPs to assist region's country teams
Country team	Ability to request and manage assets for multiple missions SDO "command-like" authority JTF-like structure	Country team manpower sensitivities; over-militarization of embassies	Better cross-training between services and agencies Staff training for semi-operational role	TTPs for close cooperation with country team staff

Summary

The institutional implications of developing a full-fledged Option C capability within the U.S. military are significant. That said, our brief historical analysis of past COIN and FID operations indicates that a full-fledged Option C capability is probably not needed, or even appropriate, in every situation where the U.S. decides to support a partner government facing an insurgency. Although it is risky to generalize from a small number of cases, U.S. involvement in countering insurgencies in South Vietnam, El Salvador, and Colombia in the 1950s–1970s,

1980s, and 1990s to the present, respectively, suggests a menu of "shape and assist" options depending on the level of partner political-military difficulty and the extent of U.S. military intervention in the host country. In cases where the insurgency is entrenched and widespread and U.S. forces are directly involved in COIN operations (as was the case in Vietnam), the SDO may require full tactical control over all military activities. The U.S. government's SC/TAA structure could extend throughout the host nation country and military, and its mission might include reform of the security sector as well as the full range of SC/TAA tasks. Such complex cases may necessitate a cadre of advisors with professional-level technical and specialized training, who remain in country for more than a year. Very tight civil-military coordination will probably be required. In most cases, this will entail military and civilian agencies falling under the direct control of the ambassador.

For intermediate FID cases similar to Colombia and, to a certain extent El Salvador, the SDO probably should be recognized as the "supported" commander by U.S. military elements in the host country. The SAO could encompass unit-level or geographic advisory teams. The U.S. Mission could include strategic (e.g., political-military) and tactical-level SC/TAA. SAO personnel should have several months of language and appropriate cultural training and spend at least one year in the country. Finally, all military and civilian agencies should be at least loosely integrated within the country team.

For FID cases that are less difficult than El Salvador was for the United States by the mid-1980s, the SDO could have limited control over in-country military personnel. The SAO could be supplemented, as necessary, with MTTs and out-of-country support elements. The mission would be limited to advice on structural issues and the train-and-equip mission. Limited country-specific training would be required of SAO personnel, who might remain in the host nation for less than a year. A lesser degree of civil-military organization could be tolerated. Military and civilian agencies may even act autonomously in certain areas.

CHAPTER SIX

Findings and Implications

Summary of Findings

The RAND research team found that organizations that currently manage security cooperation (Title 10 U.S.C.) and security assistance (Title 22 U.S.C.) work relatively well in most countries where peacetime engagement is the norm. Many sources refer to these organizations collectively as performing "security cooperation" and we will follow this practice, differentiating between them only when needed for clarity. In particular, if security cooperation efforts can be planned in advance and there is no need for significant changes during a given budget year, current practices and authorities suffice. However, as we detail below, there is room for improvement. When unbudgeted requirements arise during a fiscal year, whether they are new programs or significant changes to existing programs, the current system presents difficulties, due to inflexible authorities and funding mechanisms, as well as sometimes less-than-ideal interagency coordination.

During peacetime operations, personnel at the country, regional, and Washington levels can often deal with these structural problems successfully when they work to foster good interagency coordination and cooperation. We have presented examples of successful efforts in this report.

However, the lessons gained through these successful security cooperation efforts are seldom captured and institutionalized. Doing so would provide better coordination at the country team level (horizontal integration), as well as among the layers of security cooperation organizations—from country team to Washington, D.C. (vertical integration). Adopting these good practices would require no changes in authorities or structure, though it would require cooperation on the part of the services and the departments of State and Defense.

To go beyond the status quo, two distinct sets of changes are needed. First, new or modified legal authorities and funding mechanisms will be required to increase flexibility, particularly within a given fiscal year. To create this flexibility, Congress would need to enact changes to existing authorities or create new authorities that govern and fund security cooperation. Legislation modeled on the Stafford Act, which provides authorities and appropriations for government agencies to react to domestic emergencies, should be considered. This would include the ability to move funds from one appropriation category to another and to fund increasingly challenging types of programs: equipping, training on nonlethal and lethal techniques, and broad security force development. There would be firmly established criteria to define when these authorities could be invoked. If such a statute were not passed, or if gaps still existed after it had been passed, DoD should draft legislation to address these shortfalls and coordinate it with Congress, so that it could be ready in times of emergency. This would

39

significantly cut down on the time required to pass needed legislation in times of emergency. Finally, in rare cases, the President might have authority to take needed emergency actions inherent in his or her constitutional role. If this is determined to be necessary, then Executive Orders could be prepared for signature to activate those authorities.

Second, to improve the management of both security cooperation and relationships with the host nation in demanding circumstances short of the deployment of larger U.S. forces, the SDO needs the authority to manage all U.S. security cooperation and TAA efforts in theater. The provision of foreign internal defense is a good example of the kind of activity that would benefit from the SDO having this kind of authority (as well as the training to successfully do so). Only in a few countries would such arrangements be needed. This authority would need to be formally provided and made clear to all operating in a host nation. A DoD Directive could provide that authority, and it could be written into deployment and operations orders for all military units and teams being sent to a given country.

Although the Army may have limited influence on the willingness of Congress to enact these legal changes, it can focus its efforts on building the institutional capability and capacity to support the transition from normal, peacetime security cooperation to a country team's efforts at training, advising, and assisting a foreign country in a crisis situation.

In particular, the SDO in selected countries needs to be able to manage U.S. efforts to support foreign internal defense or other military/security operations, short of active participation as a deployed force in COIN or stability operations. To do this, the Army should improve its ability to supply security cooperation managers, trainers, advisors, and direct assistance for FID-like missions, in close cooperation with the RCCs and the State Department. This implies the ability to field trained SC/TAA personnel in larger numbers than currently provided, particularly if the SAO is managing large efforts, such as during FID. This, in turn, implies the need for programs to recruit, retain, and develop such capabilities. Although this is a joint mission and the Army need not be the executive agent—indeed, recent decisions have given U.S. Special Operations Command the lead on doctrine and training for TAA—the Army and the other services will need to provide professionals in the right numbers and with the right skills. This is a Title 10 service responsibility.

Furthermore, there will be many requirements for units or personnel to perform SC/TAA missions that are temporary—that is, outside of providing trained personnel for SAO duty. Military training teams and SATMO technical advisors are good examples of this requirement.

Although U.S. Special Operations Command has been given the lead for joint doctrine, Army doctrine may also be needed. A close look at how the Army and ASCCs manage SC/TAA missions and doctrinal implications is called for.

Finally, security cooperation lessons learned should be captured and used to develop everything from legislative proposals (e.g., on making 1206 authority permanent), to doctrine and organizational structure. The Army Center for Army Lessons Learned is the ideal organization for this task.

Summary of Implications

Our research indicates that efficiencies can be achieved in "Option A" with improved and institutionalized cooperation, coordination, and training, based on evidence of changes already made by country teams and their supporting organizations up through Washington, D.C.

However, additional gains could be made with changes to existing authorities or the introduction of new ones, along with associated spending for security cooperation and security assistance activities. Finally, for a small number of countries that are important to the U.S. and are under significant pressure, additional capabilities to provide SC/TAA assistance would greatly improve the U.S. ability to provide assistance.

This research also shows that the Army plays a central role in most of these changes. As the service with the largest number of security assistance officers and a robust training and preparatory role in security cooperation, the Army should provide intellectual leadership in the realm of policy proposals and idea generation. In particular, should Option C be adopted, the Army is a logical choice to create ways to supply trainers, advisors, and direct assistance personnel; help develop a regional joint and interagency organization that can accept the incoming supply of DoD personnel; and tailor teams that will, in turn, support the embassy and the partner nation.

We summarize the full range of implications of all three options in Table 6.1 (this table consolidates the material in Tables 3.1, 4.1, and 5.1 in one place for ease of reference). Note that Options A and B articulate changes that could be categorized as general—that is, they should be either adopted or available if circumstances demand, and would be implemented in, or available to, all SAOs worldwide. However, the full suite of changes presented in Option C would be needed in only a small number of countries.

Table 6.1
Summary of Implications for Options A, B, and C

Level	Organization	Manpower	Training	Doctrine
Washington, D.C.	Interagency security cooperation teams in Washington, D.C. Propose changes in authorities	Possible enhancements to USAID, State, other government agencies. DoD policy on loaned manpower to civilian agencies for security cooperation tasks	SAO training for security cooperation personnel in all services and agencies	Joint and interagency doctrine and concepts related to security cooperation and political-military consideration. Presidential directives on regional interagency organizations. Explore "pocket" authorities options
Army	Capability to generate TAA assets. Training-based security cooperation lessons learned. Support changes in authorities. Study 1206 effectiveness	Full spectrum of TAA Army and general skills. Career field implications. Numbers dependent on requirements	Training for some interservice/ interagency personnel. Political-military skill sets	Doctrine for managing TAA up to and including FID in counterterrorism or in conjunction with JTF
Region	Interagency regional security cooperation focus	Interagency staff available to RCC	More interagency involvement in exercises with a security cooperation/ FID dimension	

Table 6.1—Continued

Level	Organization	Manpower	Training	Doctrine
ASCC	Develop capability to participate in vertically integrated security cooperation efforts Ability to coordinate and support security cooperation/TAA assets in regional countries	Establish cadre of SC/TAA administrators	Train ASCC personnel in security cooperation Improve political-military skills, language, and cultural awareness of SC/TAA personnel Improve political-military skills, language, and cultural awareness of SC/TAA personnel	TTPs and SOPs for assisting SAO with Army security cooperation programs
Country team	Functional working groups for key areas Ability to request and manage assets for multiple missions SDO "command-like" authority	Country team manpower sensitivities; over-militarization of embassies	Better cross-training between services and agencies Staff training for semi-operational role	TTPs for close cooperation with country team staff

Case Studies

The case studies presented below support the discussion in Chapter Three. Key points are summarized in Table A.1.

The "Team Ukraine" Model

Team Ukraine, which was started in 2000, was a network of interagency professionals focused on a common set of agreed-upon objectives aimed at promoting U.S.-Ukraine political-military relations. Team Ukraine was an ad hoc arrangement among DoD, State Department, and intelligence community officials. Specifically, the following offices were incorporated into Team Ukraine: OSD/Policy (Russia, Ukraine, Eurasia office and NATO Policy); Joint Staff/ Russia, Ukraine, Eurasia; Office of Defense Cooperation Kyiv; DAO Kyiv; U.S. European Command (EUCOM) ECJ5; the Defense Security Cooperation Agency (DSCA) Ukraine Country Desk; U.S. Army Europe; Defense Intelligence Agency Ukraine Country Desk; Central Intelligence Agency, Ukraine Country Desk; State Department, Political-Military Affairs; State Department, Europe/Eurasia Coordinator's Office; and the NATO Military Liaison

Table A.1
Case Studies of Security Cooperation in Peacetime

Country	Context			Organizational Solution	
Ukraine	Well-coordinated security cooperation approach	Important relationship with host nation—combined strategic plan	Interagency Working Group	Coordination by agencies at country, regional, and national levels	Replicated, but not institutionalized
Georgia	Focus on training and equipping	Important relationship with host nation—combined strategic plan	Interagency initiative (16 sources of programs and funds)	In-country, national, and multinational coordination	Ad hoc model, but somewhat similar to other TEPs
Thailand and the Philippines	Comprehensive security cooperation	Established, but difficult relationship with host nation		JUSMAG	In-country interagency coordination

Mission, Kyiv. The concept was eventually shared and agreed upon with Ukrainian counterparts in the Ministry of Defense and the General Staff.

One of the most interesting aspects of Team Ukraine was that interagency counterparts at the action officer level, led by the OSD, came together to draft a "Joint U.S.-Ukraine Action Plan" that aligned security cooperation ends, ways, and means. All activities conducted with Ukraine—including, for example, noncommissioned officer training, National Guard State Partnership Program events, EUCOM Joint Contact Team Program familiarization events, State Department security assistance, intelligence cooperation agreements, and many others—were all incorporated, tracked, and resourced within the Action Plan.

As a team, counterparts pared down 25 objectives to five key prioritized objectives. All agencies agreed on these five key objectives, and as a result, efforts were made to align all activities with at least one key objective. Activities were resourceable, as verified by the State Department, and assessed using time lines to show progress.

Counterparts from the interagency Team Ukraine process formally met several times annually at several events including the EUCOM Regional Working Group (later renamed the Theater Security Cooperation Working Group) in October, the OSD/Joint Staff Eurasia Policy and Strategy Conference in January and February, and the OSD Bilateral Working Group (later renamed the Bilateral Defense Cooperation talks) with the Ukrainians, held approximately every six months. The Ukrainian Chief of Defense signed the Joint Action Plan, as did the Assistant Secretary of Defense. These planning events, whether U.S.-only or with Ukraine, provided Team Ukraine an opportunity to physically meet to discuss progress made in the Action Plan, upcoming events, measures of effectiveness, resourcing issues, and political developments. In between events, Ukraine had a virtual network, connected by the SIPRnet, to discuss everyday issues. The Joint Action Plan was updated monthly as a result of current developments.

Team Ukraine flourished for two main reasons. First, the political climate was ripe for working with Ukraine in a capacity-building context: President Kuchma was seen as a favorable political leader between 1997 and 2002. Second, U.S. counterparts at the action officer level agreed to work together in pursuit of common objectives.[1]

This ad hoc arrangement lasted about four years, until all the original Team Ukraine members eventually changed positions. Interestingly, the Georgian country director in OSD/Eurasia tried to emulate the model and was quite successful. The same fate befell "Team Georgia" after the original members eventually moved on to other positions. However, Georgia was the recipient of one of the first-ever interagency train-and-equip programs, which served to encourage effective coordination among interagency stakeholders.

The Georgia Train and Equip Program

The Georgia Train and Equip Program (GTEP) did not have exactly the same sense of interagency team-building experience as Team Ukraine did, but the circumstances were different.

GTEP was a presidentially directed program of assistance to the military and other security services of Georgia. In 1999, U.S. President Bill Clinton and Georgian President Eduard Shevardnadze agreed upon a large-scale capacity-building program for Georgia in an effort to

---

[1]   Author observations as a participant in this process.

root out terrorists in the Pankisi Gorge region in Georgia. GTEP, which officially began in May 2002, totaled $64 million and incorporated 16 different funding sources from various security cooperation programs overseen and executed by the State Department and the Department of Defense. These funding sources included the State Department's Foreign Military Financing program, the International Military Education and Training program, the Georgia Border Security and Law Enforcement program, the Anti-Terrorism Assistance program, and several others. From DoD, programs such as the Cooperative Threat Reduction's Proliferation Prevention Program, the DTRA International Counterproliferation Program, the National Guard State Partnership Program, and the Counter-Terrorism Fellowship Program were included in the broader GTEP.

GTEP originally began as a counterterrorism-focused endeavor but was transformed into a coalition support program in 2004. Interagency working groups, led by the State Department' Coordinator's office, were created to support GTEP, given the complexities of pooling resources from many different funding sources.

Similar to the Team Ukraine model, Georgia was determined to be a priority country in Eurasia for State Department and DoD engagement. As such, the political climate supported the deepening of security cooperation with Georgia. Interestingly, GTEP eventually included key allies, the UK in particular, as providers of peacekeeping exercises to test GTEP-acquired capabilities. GTEP energized interagency coordination and deconfliction in Washington, Germany (EUCOM and USAREUR), and in Tbilisi.

GTEP really forced interagency cooperation on a single-country train and equip program primarily because it was presidentially mandated and directed, though not centrally funded. Essentially, GTEP embodies U.S. government security cooperation at its best; that is, disparate actors coming together to promote a single country-specific train and equip, with clear objectives, pooled resources, and metrics to assess success over time.

As with Team Ukraine, interagency counterparts had an opportunity to meet roughly three times per year, at the EUCOM Theater Security Cooperation Working Group in Germany, at the OSD/Joint Staff Policy and Strategy Conference in Washington, and during talks with Georgian counterparts to reinforce key concepts and measure progress.

Philippines and Thailand: Interagency Cooperation in the JUSMAG

In addition to the three previous models of interagency cooperation in the Eurasia region, the Asia-Pacific region provides some interesting examples of how interagency security cooperation can work successfully in practice. In both the Philippines and Thailand, as is the case in most U.S. embassies, weekly country team meetings are held with all interagency representatives, which in these cases include about 30 agencies and organizations. The goal of these meetings is to coordinate and deconflict among a variety of agencies and activities. Moreover, routine meetings are held within working groups (law enforcement, intelligence, etc.) when necessary. In addition, short-duration "Tiger Teams" have been created to help coordinate larger-scale train and equip programs. An example is the 1206 Global Train and Equip program in the Philippines. Such working group meetings and tiger teams certainly help in the coordination of security cooperation activities and ensure that security cooperation programs are centralized. The Defense Attaché's office does not have a strong role in this respect. In both the Philippines and Thailand, the JUSMAG (i.e., SAO) has the primary responsibility for security cooperation programs and activities. Specifically, the Defense Attaché's office has Title 10 responsibility only for Asia Pacific Center activities, while the JUSMAG is responsible for all other Title 10 and Title 22 security assistance.

However, insufficient interagency resources and restrictive programmatic authorities make it difficult to live up to host nation expectations in the Asia-Pacific region. Restrictive authorities limit JUSMAG's effectiveness to work with other security services. Moreover, and according to DoD in-country officials, the addition of more OSD and Pacific Command priority countries in the area of responsibility has led to a situation where "the mayonnaise is spread so thin on the bread you can hardly taste it anymore." In conclusion, four models of interagency cooperation and coordination have been presented in this section. In each case, examples of successful cooperation and deconfliction were presented. However, the political climate will continue to dictate the extent to which interagency cooperation in country can be achieved, and whether a coordinated approach at the tactical level, including Washington-based country team members, is required. It seems, however, that the more stakeholders are included in a focused capacity-building country plan, the better the U.S. government will be able to prioritize objectives, focus resources, and evaluate success.

Overview of Army Security Cooperation Programs and Authorities

This appendix contains a matrix of the major security cooperation programs of the U.S. Army, as of the completion of research (summer 2008). It is meant as a reference for practitioners, and an easily accessible guide for them. As such, no effort is made to spell out all acronyms, and significant familiarity with the field is assumed. For those who need more detailed explanations, the references provided in the right-most column should be helpful. All links were active as of November 1, 2009.

Program	Categories	Authority	Language	Source Link
Latin American Cooperation LATAM COOP	Non-training-related activity	10 U.S.C. Sec. 1050	"Pay travel, subsistence, and special compensation to officers and students." "Funds for the conduct of exchanges, seminars, conferences, briefings, orientation visits, and other similar activities are made available to each of the military departments. Military departments, in turn, distribute the funds throughout each of the departments for funding the engagement program."	http://www.law.cornell.edu/uscode/search/display.html?terms=1050&url=/uscode/html/uscode10/usc_sec_10_00001050----000-.html
Western Hemisphere, Institute for Security Cooperation (WHINSEC)	Training on nonlethal techniques	10 U.S.C. Sec. 2166	Sec Def "may operate an education and training facility for the purpose of providing professional education and training to eligible personnel of nations of the Western Hemisphere within the context of the democratic principles set forth in the Charter of the Organization of American States."	http://www.law.cornell.edu/uscode/search/display.html?terms=western%20hemisphere%20institute&url=/uscode/html/uscode10/usc_sec_10_00002166----000-.html

47

Program	Categories	Authority	Language	Source Link
Kermit Roosevelt Lecture Series	Non-training-related activity	AR 37-47	Authorized the Kermit Roosevelt Fund and established in the "War Department" a Board of Trustees to implement and administer the exchange program "for the purpose of fostering a better understanding and a closer relationship between the military forces of the United States and those of the United Kingdom by sponsoring lectures or courses of instruction."	http://www-cgsc.army. mil/carl/resources/archival/ kermit.asp
International Center for Research and Development	Non–training related activity	10 U.S.C. Sec. 2371, P.L. 99-502, EO 12591, 15 U.S.C. Sec. 3710a	An International Other Transaction (OT), authorized by 10 U.S.C. 2371, is available for use with foreign nongovernment entities, primarily industries and universities, and may be considered along with contracts and IAs during the development of an acquisition strategy. Nondomestic Cooperative Research and Development Agreements (CRADAs) authorized by 15 U.S.C. 3710a enable the U.S. to benefit from scientific technology developed abroad.	http://www.law.cornell. edu/uscode/search/display. html?terms=2371%20&url=/ uscode/html/uscode10/ usc_sec_10_00002371---- 000-.html
Institutional training and education of foreign militaries and selected civilians	Training on nonlethal techniques, equipment	(See FMF, FMS, IMET, EDA, Drawdowns, Exchanges, INCLE, ACRI, EIPC— all funded by Foreign National Funds. For DoD funded programs Regional Centers for Security Studies)	DoS page, covers all FA programs and therefore include all FA authorities.	http://www.state.gov/t/pm/ rls/rpt/fmtrpt/2002/10607. htm

Program	Categories	Authority	Language	Source Link
Exchange-Engineer & Scientist Exchange Program	Non-training-related activity	National Defense Authorization Act for Fiscal Year 1997, Sec. 1082; 10 U.S.C. 168 note; P.L. 104-201	"authority to enter into international exchange agreements. Secretary of Defense may enter into international defense personnel exchange agreements. Personnel may be assigned to positions in defense ministry of such foreign government."	http://www.govtrack.us/congress/bill.xpd?bill=h109-5122&tab=summary
Senior National Representative (Army) (SNRA)	Non-training-related activity	10 U.S.C., Sec. 2350a	"Enter into a memorandum of understanding (or other formal agreement) with one or more countries or organizations from NATO, major non-NATO ally, or any other friendly foreign country for the purpose of conducting cooperative research and development projects on defense equipment and munitions."	http://www.law.cornell.edu/uscode/10/usc_sec_10_00002350---a000-.html
EDA	Equipment	22 U.S.C. Sec. 2321j; 2318 (also known as Section 506 of the FAA); Sec. 2348a, (also known as Section 552 of the FAA, P.L. 87-195).	Sell defense articles and defense services from the stocks of the Department of Defense to any eligible country or international organization if such country or international organization agrees to pay in U.S. dollars (U.S.C. 2761); Transfer excess defense articles to countries for which receipt of such articles was justified pursuant to the annual congressional presentation documents for military assistance programs. (U.S.C. 2321j)	http://www.law.cornell.edu/uscode/22/2321j.html

Program	Categories	Authority	Language	Source Link
FMS	Equipment, Training on lethal and nonlethal techniques (as relates to equipment)	22 U.S.C. Ch. 39, Sec. 2763; AECA (Arms Export Control Act)	Finance procurement of defense articles, defense services, and design & construction services by friendly foreign countries & int'l organizations (U.S.C. 2763); provide financing to Israel & Egypt for the procurement by leasing defense articles from US commercial suppliers (U.S.C. 2763); charge interest at such a rate as he may determine, except not be less than 5% per year (U.S.C. 2763); conduct audits on a nonreimbursable basis of private firms that have entered into contracts with foreign governments (US.C. 2763).	http://www.law.cornell.edu/uscode/22/usc_sup_01_22_10_39_20_II.html
Leases of Defense Articles	Equipment	22 U.S.C. 2796, also known as Chapter 6, AECA (P.L. 90-269)	"Lease defense articles in the stocks of the Department of Defense to an eligible foreign country or international organization."	http://www.law.cornell.edu/uscode/search/display.html?terms=leases%20defense%20articles&url=/uscode/html/uscode22/usc_sec_22_00002796----000-.html
Army War College Int'l Fellows Program	Non–training related activity	Title 10, Subtitle B, Part III, Chapter 403	Each year approximately 40 senior military officers from 40 different countries are extended an invitation from the Chief of Staff of the United States Army to attend the U.S. Army War College. The academic year is full of studying, research, and fellowship as these officers are exposed to and instructed in areas ranging from military concepts and doctrine to national- and theater-level strategies.	http://www.law.cornell.edu/uscode/search/display.html?terms=%20exchange%20program&url=/uscode/html/uscode10/usc_sec_10_00004345----000-.html
Command & General Staff College Int'l Fellows Program	Non-training-related activity	AR 12-15 Joint Security Assistance Training Regulation para 1–4	Provide fellowships to selected senior Army officers from allied and other friendly nations.	http://www.army.mil/usapa/epubs/pdf/r12_15.pdf

Program	Categories	Authority	Language	Source Link
Schools of Other Nations	Non-training-related activity	Section 544 of the FAA, also known as Sec. 2347c of Title 22, U.S. Code	U.S. officers participating in the Schools of Other Nations program attend a foreign military school and get credit for courses attended.	http://www.usaid.gov/policy/ads/faa.pdf
SCT Teams (or Security Assistance Team)	Non-training-related activity	No specific authority	PM/PPA's Security Assistance Team develops military assistance policy and manages security assistance funding through three programs: Foreign Military Financing (FMF), International Military Education and Training (IMET), and Peacekeeping Operations (PKO). Determines military assistance policy, develops and manages the programs' budgets, provides notifications to Congress, supports determinations made to waive legislative constraints on security assistance funding, distributes funds, and provides program oversight. Additionally, PM/PPA coordinates and implements State Department participation in the new Defense Department authority (Sec. 1206) that provides DoD with resources to build the capacity of global partners to respond to emergent needs and challenges.	http://www.state.gov/t/pm/ppa/sat/

Program	Categories	Authority	Language	Source Link
Sergeants Major Academy International Military Students	Training on nonlethal techniques	Title 10—Armed Forces Subtitle B—Army Part III—Training Chapter 403—U.S. Military Academy	The mission of the International Military Student Office (IMSO) is to create the conditions and climate for sustained professional growth and success; provide and coordinate support for the world's best international military students and promote a favorable impression of the American way of life; and to support the Security Assistance Training Program objectives.	http://www.law.cornell. edu/uscode/search/ display.html?terms=%20 exchange%20 program&url=/uscode/ html/uscode10/usc_ sec_10_00004345----000-. html
USMA Foreign Academy Exchange Program (FAEP)	Non-training-related activity	Title 10—Armed Forces Subtitle B, Army Part III—Training Chapter 403—U.S. Military Academy	The FAEP started in 1958 with a cadet exchange between the U.S. and Mexico. Now the program has grown to include 36 countries.	http://www.usma.edu/ PublicAffairs/PV/040430/ foreign.htm
USMA Int'l Cadet Program	Non-training-related activity	Title 10—Armed Forces Subtitle B—Army Part III—Training Chapter 403—U.S. Military Academy	All non-U.S. citizens interested in applying for Admission to the United States Military Academy at West Point are first advised to contact the U.S. Defense Attaché Office located at the American Embassy in their native country. The USDAO serves as the link between the student, the host nation, and the United States Military Academy. Revision of Title X of the U.S. Code in 1963 authorized up to sixty International Cadets to study at USMA at any given time. Eligible countries are selected on an annual basis by the U.S. State Department and the U.S. Department of Defense.	http://www.law.cornell. edu/uscode/search/ display.html?terms=%20 exchange%20 program&url=/uscode/ html/uscode10/usc_ sec_10_00004345----000-. html

Program	Categories	Authority	Language	Source Link
The USMA Study Abroad Program	Non-training-related activity	Title 10—Armed Forces Subtitle B—Army Part III—Training Chapter 403—United States Military Academy; 10 U.S.C. 4345	Permit student enrolled at a military academy of a foreign country to receive instruction at the Academy in exchange for a cadet receiving instruction at that foreign military academy pursuant to an exchange agreement entered into between the Secretary and appropriate officials of the foreign country—10 U.S.C. 4345	http://www.law.cornell.edu/uscode/search/display.html?terms=exchange&url=/uscode/html/uscode10/usc_sec_10_00004345----000-.html
Administrative & Professionals Exchange Program (APEP)	Non-training-related activity	National Defense Authorization Act Fiscal Year 1997, Sec. 1082; 10 U.S.C. 168 Note	Exchange of Army career administrators and professionals in fields like administration, finance, legal, planning	http://thomas.loc.gov/cgi-bin/query/z?c104:hr.3230.enr:
Engineer & Scientist Exchange Program	Non-training-related activity	DoD Directive 5230.20; National Defense Authorization Act Fiscal Year 1997, Sec. 1082; 10 U.S.C. 168 note	Provide career broadening work assignments to foreign personnel in U.S. defense establishments and for U.S. defense personnel in foreign defense establishments. Central funding to assist organizations in covering costs (PCS/TDY, language training, etc.) to place U.S. Army participants abroad.	www.dami.army.pentagon.mil/pub/dami-fd/5230-20.pdf

Program	Categories	Authority	Language	Source Link
Foreign Liaison Officers (FLO)	Non-training-related activity	AR 380-10	The Army Foreign Liaison Officer Program was established to facilitate cooperation and mutual understanding between U.S. Army and armies of allied and friendly nations. A FLO is a foreign government military member or civilian employee who is authorized by his or her government, and is certified by a DA component in connection with programs, projects, or agreements of interest to the governments.	http://www.dami.army.pentagon.mil/offices/dami-cd/flo.asp
Military Personnel Exchange Program (MPEP)	Non-training-related activity	DoD Directive 5230.20	MPEP is an instrument … to build, sustain, and expand international relationships that are critical enablers.	http://www.dtic.mil/whs/directives/corres/html/523020.htm
Reciprocal Unit Exchange (RUE)	Training on nonlethal techniques	22 U.S.C. 2770a	"Provide training and related support to military and civilian defense personnel of a friendly foreign country or an international organization. Such training and related support may include the provision of transportation, food services, health services, and logistics and the use of facilities and equipment."	http://www.law.cornell.edu/uscode/search/display.html?terms=2770a&url=/uscode/html/uscode22/usc_sec_22_00002770---a000-.html
Reserve Individuals Exchange	Training on nonlethal techniques	DoD Directive 1215.15	Provided National Guard and Reserve Officers training associated with mobilization duties while working with host nation.	http://www.defenselink.mil/ra/html/rofe.html

Program	Categories	Authority	Language	Source Link
Army-to-Army Staff Talks	Non-training-related activity	AR 34-1	Only forum that covers the full spectrum of Security Cooperation issues and are the primary Army medium for the development of interoperability with strategic partners. Staff Talks focus on doctrine, training, and education, materiel and equipment, and logistics.	http://www.army.mil/usapa/ epubs/34_Series_Collection_1. html
Center for Army Lessons Learned—Int'l Engagements	Non-training-related activity	AR 11-33	The Center for Army Lessons Learned (CALL) collects and analyzes data from a variety of current and historical sources, including Army operations and training events, and produces lessons for military commanders, staff, and students.	http://call.army.mil/#
Civil-Military Emergency Preparedness	Training on nonlethal techniques	42 U.S.C. 5195; 10 U.S.C. 113	Provide system of emergency preparedness for protection of life and property in the United States from hazards and to vest responsibility for emergency preparedness jointly in the Federal Government and the States and their political subdivisions. Provide necessary direction, coordination, and guidance, and shall provide necessary assistance.	http://www.law.cornell.edu/ uscode/html/uscode42/usc_ sec_42_00005195----000-.html
CSA Counterpart Visit Program	Non-training-related activity	AR 37-47	Host visits to the U.S. by CSA's counterparts from key countries; includes CSA's visits to counterparts in their countries.	http://www.usma.army.mil/ Protocol/army_regs.htm

Program	Categories	Authority	Language	Source Link
Distinguished Foreign Visits	Non-training-related activity	22 U.S.C., 2452	Provide educational exchanges, (i) by financing studies, research, instruction, and other educational activities—of or for American citizens and nationals in foreign countries or for citizens and nationals of foreign countries in American schools and institutions of learning located in or outside the United States; and (ii) by financing visits and interchanges between the United States and other countries of students, trainees, teachers, instructors, and professors.	http://www.law.cornell.edu/uscode/22/usc_sec_22_00002452----000-.html
Foreign Area Officer In-Country Training	Training on nonlethal techniques	DA Pam 600-3; DoDD 5105.75	Qualified officers selected to attend foreign schools; AR 350-1 contains list of foreign schools that U.S. officers attend; FAOS commissioned officers deliberately accessed, trained, educated, and developed to increase their strategic focus, regional expertise, foreign language proficiency, and professional military skills and experience.	www.usapa.army.mil/pdffiles/p600_3.pdf
Foreign Attaché Orientation Program	Non-training-related activity	DoDD 5230.20; DoDD 5105.75	Provide necessary training to officers selected as the SDO/defense attaché to function as the principle DoD representative on the Country Team responsible for providing coordinated views on all DoD matters.	www.dtic.mil/whs/directives/corres/pdf/510575p.pdf
National Guard Bureau–State Partnership Program (NGB-SPP)	Training on nonlethal techniques	National Defense Authorization Act 1993 (yearly)	To link U.S. states with partner countries.	thomas.loc.gov/cgi-bin/query/z?c102:H.R.5006.ENR

Program	Categories	Authority	Language	Source Link
Training & Doctrine Conferences (TDC)	Non-training-related activity	AR 34-1, Multinational Force Compatibility AR 11-31, Army International Security Cooperation, Policy Army Security Cooperation Plan	TRADOC initiative that was developed as a follow-on to TRADOC's relinquishing of executive agency for DA Staff Talks.	www.armystudyguide.com/content/publications/army_regulations/ar-1131.shtml
European Security Agreements	Non-training-related activity Training on nonlethal techniques, Equipment	Overall regulations: Army Europe Regulation 525-50; DoD Directives 2060.1, 2060.2, 5530.3; CJCSI 2300.01D; NSPD 17; NSPD 20. For the WMD Nonproliferation Agreement Implementation program: Chemical Weapons Convention, CJCSI 2030.01B; 22 U.S.C. 2593a; 22 U.S.C. 6728	AE Regulation 350-1: Prioritize military training requirements from the individual soldier to the JTF level; provide guidance on how units in the Army in Europe train with joint, multinational, and emerging coalition partners in a joint, coalition, warfighting environment; synchronize training requirements outlined in other Army in Europe training publications and training policy in Army in Europe command policy letters; provide training strategy based on leveraging available training resources.	www.hqusareur.army.mil/htmlinks/Press_Releases/AER350-1.pdf
WMD Nonproliferation Agreement Implementation	Non-training-related activity	The Treaty on the Non-Proliferation of Nuclear Weapons	"Considering the devastation that would be visited upon all mankind by a nuclear war and the consequent need to make every effort to avert the danger of such a war and to take measures to safeguard the security of peoples, "Believing that the proliferation of nuclear weapons would seriously enhance the danger of nuclear war."	http://www.un.org/Depts/dda/WMD/treaty/

Program	Categories	Authority	Language	Source Link
DASA(R&T)/Chief Scientist Forums	Non-training-related activity	AR 70-41; 10 U.S.C. 2538b; 10 U.S.C. 2350a; National Defense Authorization Act 1997, Sec. 1082	10 U.S.C. 2539b permits DoD laboratories to all testing services of the states, private sector, and foreign entities. 10 U.S.C. 2350a provides authority to conduct cooperative R&D projects on defense equipment and munitions with NATO organizations, members of NATO, and major non-NATO allies. The NDAA 1997 provides authority to negotiate agreements with allies or other friendly foreign countries to exchange military and civilian DoD personnel with military and civilian personnel of foreign defense ministries.	http://www.army.mil/usapa/epubs/pdf/r70_41.pdf
Foreign Comparative Testing (FCT)	Equipment, Non-training-related activity	Title 10 2360a(g), AFI 16-110	"…Secretary of Defense should test conventional defense equipment, munitions, and technologies manufactured and developed by countries referred to in Subsect. (a)(2) to determine the ability of such equipment, munitions, and technologies to satisfy U.S. military requirements or to correct operational deficiencies; and that while the testing of nondevelopmental items and items in the late state of the development process are preferred, the testing of equipment, munitions, and technologies may be conducted to determine procurement alternatives."	http://www.acq.osd.mil/cto/handbook/OSD_CTO_Procedures_Handbook_v1.pdf

Program	Categories	Authority	Language	Source Link
Int'l Technology Centers	Non-training-related activity	AR 70-41	To support the identification, acquisition, integration, and delivery of foreign technology solutions to the warfighter to ensure technological superiority on the battlefield.	http://www.usaitca.army.mil/
Loans of Defense Equipment (Section 65)	Equipment	22 U.S.C. 2796d, AFI 16-110	22 USC 2796d states that the military services may conclude and implement written agreements to make, accept, and administer loans, without charge, of U.S. defense materials, supplies, or equipment to, and to accept loans or gifts of defense materials, supplies, or equipment from NATO and major non-NATO allies. These agreements permit no-cost loan of equipment for the purposes of cooperative research, development, test, or evaluation programs.	www.e-publishing.af.mil/shared/media/epubs/AFI16-110.pdf
The Research & Technology Board (RTB)	Non-training-related activity	NATO organization under the authorization Treaty (North Atlantic Treaty Organization—NATO)	The Research & Technology Board (RTB) constitutes the highest authority within the Research and Technology Organization (RTO), and is the policy body tasked by the North Atlantic Counsel (NAC) through the Conference of National Armaments Directors (CNAD) and Military Committee (MC) to carry out the mission of the RTO.	http://www.rta.nato.int/panel.asp?panel=RTB

Program	Categories	Authority	Language	Source Link
Multilateral Interoperability Program (MIP)	Non-training-related activity	The MIP came about in 2001 by merging two previous separate programs: The "Army Tactical Command and Control Information System" (ATCCIS) and the former MIP.	The MIP specification is a managed interface between C2 information systems. When incorporated into a system, it enables interoperability of information between any other system that also incorporates the specification. Battlespace data is transferred as information. The meaning and context of the information is preserved across national boundaries precisely and without any ambiguity.	http://www.mip-site.org/020_Public_History.htm

Program	Categories	Authority	Language	Source Link
NATO Army Armaments Group (NAAG)	Non-training-related activity	U.S. Authorities: 1. DoDD 5134.01 www.dtic. mil/whs/ directives/corres/ pdf/513401p.pdf 2. AR70-41 2-2. ASAALT, (g) appoints the Army rep. to the NATO Army Armaments Group and Five Power Senior National Representatives (Army) SNR(A) forums. 3. OUSD AT&L/ Int'l Cooperation Handbook ID's DASA DE&C as NAAG rep (pg 19, 3.3.1).	The NATO Army Armaments Group (NAAG) is one of the three Main Armament Groups subordinate to the Conference of National Armaments Director (CNAD). The CNAD in turn reports directly to the North Atlantic Council (NAC), the ultimate authority in NATO. The CNAD for the U.S. is the OUSD AT&L. In this capacity, the USD (AT&L) shall: 3.31. Serve as the National Armaments Director (NAD) at the North Atlantic Treaty Organization (NATO) Conference of National Armaments Directors (CNAD) and in other similar NAD-level multilateral and bilateral fora. Establish and publish policies and procedures governing DoD Acquisition System activities in support of the CNAD, the Senior NATO Logisticians Conference, the NATO Research and Technology Organization, and other similar multilateral or bilateral fora.	www.nato.int/structur/ AC/225/225ENG/naaghome. htm
NATO Standardization Agency	Non-training-related activity	?	The mission of the NSA is to initiate, co-ordinate, support, and administer standardization activities conducted under the authority of the NATO Committee for Standardization (NCS).	http://www.nato.int/nsa/ nsa_home.htm

Program	Categories	Authority	Language	Source Link
ABCA Armies Program	Non-training-related activity	Ratification of the Basic Standardization Agreement 1964 (BSA 64)	The focus of the Program is on interoperability, defined as: the ability of Alliance Forces, and when appropriate, forces of Partner and other Nations, to train, exercise, and operate effectively together in the execution of assigned missions and tasks. Member countries acknowledge that future operations are likely to be in coalition with ABCA and other willing nations. Methods of improving, testing, and enhancing coalition processes, procedures, and systems in peacetime are likely to optimize coalition interoperability on operations.	http://www.abca-armies. org/History/Default.aspx
Int'l Medical Programs—Army Medical Dept. (AMEDD)	Non-training-related activity	No specific authority	Includes management of Reciprocal Healthcare Agreements, NATO/ Partnership for Peace, Medical Eligibility Charts, and Army Medical Treatment Facilities. Additionally, AMEDD International Programs provide travel information including entry requirements and travel warnings.	http://www.armymedicine. army.mil/hc/ip/intl_prgms. htm

Program	Categories	Authority	Language	Source Link
U.S. Army Corps of Engineers Int'l Activities (USACE IAP)	Non-training-related activity	Water Resources Development Act (WRDA), Sec. 234 (33 U.S.C. 2323(a); and the Foreign Assistance Action, Sec. 607 (22 U.S.C. 2357); Arms Export Control Act authority for FMS. Also the Economy Act and Sec. 632a and 632b of the Foreign Assistance Act, which are the authorities for support to USAID and the State Department.	The Corps provides engineering and construction services, environmental restoration and management services, research and development assistance, management of water and land-related natural resources, relief and recovery work, and other management and technical services.	http://www.hq.usace.army.mil/
Partnership for Peace Program	Training on nonlethal techniques, Equipment	National Defense Authorization Act (yearly) (P.L. 109-163)	Provide logistic support, supplies, and services to allied forces that are participating in active hostilities, a contingency, or a noncombat operation alongside U.S. forces in a combined operation. (It also) focus on interoperability of logistical support systems. (And) to provide humanitarian and civic assistance in conjunction with military operations and (to provide) communications or information systems equipment or supplies.	www.dod.mil/dodgc/olc/docs/PL109-163.pdf
DoD Counterdrug Operations	Training on nonlethal techniques, Equipment	P.L. 101-510, Sec. 1004, under the National Defense Authorization Act and P.L. 105-85, Sec. 1033	Provide support for the counter-drug activities (assistance and training) of any other department or agency of the Federal Government or of the State, local, or foreign law enforcement agency (S 1004).	www.dod.mil/dodgc/olc/docs/1998NDAA.pdf

Program	Categories	Authority	Language	Source Link
Cooperative Threat Reduction Program (Nunn-Lugar Program)	Non-training-related activity	P.L. 109-289 FY 07. Initially authorized by amendment to the implementing legislation for the Conventional Armed Forces in Europe (CFE) Treaty (P.L. 102-228), "Soviet Nuclear Threat Reduction Act of 1991" (commonly known as Nunn-Lugar legislation)	Soviet Nuclear Threat Reduction Act of 1991 authorized the use DoD funds to assist the Soviet Union, and its "successor entities" with efforts to "1) destroy nuclear weapons, chemical weapons, and other weapons, 2) transport, store, disable, and safeguard weapons in connection with their destruction; and 3) establish verifiable safeguards against the proliferation of such weapons." The 2004 Nunn-Lugar Expansion Act (P.L. 108-136) authorized the use of funds outside the FSU to "assist the United States in resolution of critical emerging proliferation threats and to permit the United States to take advantage of opportunities to achieve long-standing nonproliferation goals."	thomas.loc.gov/cgi-bin/query/z?c109:H.R.5631.enr:
Warsaw Pact Initiative	Non-training-related activity Training on nonlethal techniques	T 10 S168, S1051 and S2010, SAMM C11.15	T10 S168 for mil-to-mil contact, S1051 for providing assistance in attending bilateral or regional meetings, S2010 to fund participation in joint exercises.	http://www.law.cornell.edu/uscode/26/usc_sec_26_00000168----000-.html; http://www.dsca.mil/samm/
Iraq Security Forces Training (Train and Equip Iraqi Security Forces)	Training on lethal and nonlethal techniques Equipment Security Services	Title IX of DoD Appropriations Act 2007 (P.L. 109-289), Title I of Emergency Supplemental Appropriations Act 2007 (P.L. 110-28)	"...Equipping, supplying, training the Iraq Security Forces and repairing, renovating, and constructing facilities and infrastructure."	http://waysandmeans.house.gov/media/pdf/tax/HR_2206_text.pdf
Afghan Security Forces Training (Train and Equip Afghani Security Forces)	Training on lethal and nonlethal techniques Equipment Security Services	Title IX of DoD Appropriations Act 2007 (P.L. 109-289), Title I of Emergency Supplemental Appropriations Act 2007 (P.L. 110-28)	Equipping, supplying, training security forces and repairing, renovating, and constructing facilities and infrastructure.	http://waysandmeans.house.gov/media/pdf/tax/HR_2206_text.pdf

Program	Categories	Authority	Language	Source Link
Global Peace Operations Initiative	Training on lethal and nonlethal techniques Security Services	Presidential initiative utilizing authorities in 22 U.S.C. Sec. 2348-2348d; Foreign Assistance Act U.S.C. Sec. 551–554 (Chapter 6, part II of FAA and Sec. 23 of the AECA)	To provide assistance for peacekeeping operations and other programs to further U.S. national security interests "on such terms and conditions as he may determine." (FAA 551)	http://www.usaid.gov/policy/ads/faa.pdf
Foreign Disaster Assistance (ODACHA Funds)	Non-training-related activity Equipment	10 U.S.C. Sec. 404	"Provide disaster assistance outside the United States to respond to manmade or natural disasters when necessary to prevent loss of lives or serious harm to the environment." Assist foreign countries to respond to manmade or natural disaster situations when necessary to prevent loss of lives. The assistance may be in the form of transportation, excess property items, HDRs, or some other commodity.	http://www.law.cornell.edu/uscode/search/display.html?terms=404%20foreign%20disaster&url=/uscode/html/uscode10/usc_sec_10_00000404----000-.html

Program	Categories	Authority	Language	Source Link
Disaster Response Training (Humanitarian Assistance—see 2561)	Training on nonlethal techniques	10 U.S.C. Sec. 2561	"Funds authorized to be appropriated to the Department of Defense for a fiscal year for humanitarian assistance shall be used for the purpose of providing transportation of humanitarian relief and for other humanitarian purposes worldwide. transport supplies intended for use to respond to, or mitigate the effects of, an event or condition, such as an oil spill, that threatens serious harm to the environment, but only if other sources to provide such transportation are not readily available."	http://www.law.cornell. edu/uscode/10/usc_ sec_10_00002561----000-. html
Commanders Emergency Response Program (CERP)	Non-training-related activity	P.L. 109-289, Sec. 9007, Title IX	Use of up to $500 million to enable commanders in Iraq to respond to urgent humanitarian relief and reconstruction requirements. In addition, the provision requires quarterly reports to the congressional defense committees, places certain limitations on the use of funds, and requires the Secretary of Defense to issue guidance on activities eligible for funding.	http://thomas.loc. gov/cgi-bin/query/ z?c109:H.R.5631.enr:

Program	Categories	Authority	Language	Source Link
Chairman of the Joint Chiefs of Staff's Exercise Program (CJCS or CEP)	Non-training-related activity	National Defense Authorization Act for Fiscal Year 1998 (P.L. 105-85); Title 10, Sec. 153	Mix of exercises, training, maintaining relationships. Accomplish training essential to war-fighting missions first; train for lesser contingencies, such as peacekeeping and humanitarian operations, while emphasizing training for major contingencies. P.L. 105-85: Report on exercises conducted from 1995–1997 and those planned for fiscal years 1998–2000. 10 U.S.C. Sec. 153: Prepare strategic plans, including plans which conform with resource levels; prepare joint logistic and mobility plans to support those strategic plans; perform net assessments to determine capabilities of armed forces of the U.S. and its allies as compared with those of potential allies.	http://www.law.cornell.edu/uscode/10/usc_sec_10_00000153----000-.html
Developing country exercise program (DCCEP)	Training on nonlethal techniques	10 U.S.C. Sec. 2010	Authorizes payment of incremental expenses of a developing country incurred during bilateral or multilateral exercises if it enhances U.S. security interests and is essential to achieving the fundamental objectives of the exercise.(Expenses normally include rations, fuel, training ammunition, and transportation.)	http://www.law.cornell.edu/uscode/10/usc_sec_10_00002010----000-.html

Program	Categories	Authority	Language	Source Link
Joint Combined Exchange Training	Training on nonlethal techniques	10 U.S.C. Sec. 20101	...To pay the deployment and training costs of SOF training abroad with foreign security forces. DoD funding can be used for the training of foreign counterpart, expenses for the U.S. deployment and for developing countries, the incremental expenses incurred by the country for the training (such "incremental expenses" include rations, fuel, ammunition, and transportation if the host country is unable to pay).	http://www.law.cornell. edu/uscode/10/usc_ sec_10_00002011----000-. html

Program	Categories	Authority	Language	Source Link
Regional Centers for Security Studies	Non-training-related activity	Title 10, Sec. 184, NDAA of 2007, Sec. 904, DoDD 5200.41	DoD Centers for Regional Security Studies (hereafter referred to as "Regional Centers") shall support DoD policy objectives, as set forth, in particular, in the DoD Defense Strategy and the DoD Security Cooperation Guidance, with activities designed to enhance security, foster partnerships, improve national security decision-making, and strengthen civil-military relationships. This shall be accomplished through education, exchanges, research, and information sharing. A core Regional Center mission shall be to support the Department's policies and priorities by assisting military and civilian leaders in the region in developing strong defense establishments and strengthening civil-military relations in a democratic society.	http://frwebgate.access. gpo.gov/cgi-bin/getdoc. cgi?dbname=109_cong_ bills&docid=f:h5122enr.txt. pdf www.dtic.mil/whs/ directives/corres/ pdf/520041p.pdf

Program	Categories	Authority	Language	Source Link
Regional Defense Counter-Terrorism Fellowship Program	Non-training-related activity Training on nonlethal techniques	P.L. 107-117 Sec. 1825	"To pay any costs associated with the attendance of foreign military officers, ministry of defense officials, or security officials at United States military educational institutions, regional centers, conferences, seminars, or other training programs conducted under the Regional Defense Counterterrorism Fellowship Program." 2007 National Defense Authorization Act. Sec. 1024 of this bill would make "enhancements" to the CTFP, allowing funds to be used to send students to civilian educational institutions in the United States, and increasing the annual worldwide budget from $20 million to $25 million.	http://www.defenselink.mil/policy/sections/policy_offices/gsa/ctfp/index.html

Program	Categories	Authority	Language	Source Link
Presidential Drawdown	Equipment	FAA, U.S.C. Sec. 2318, 2348a	Drawdown defense articles from the stocks of DoD, defense services of DoD, and military education and training, of an aggregate value not to exceed $100,000,000 in any fiscal year (U.S.C. 2318); Exercise authority of section 2360(a) to transfer funds available to carry out military assistance, except that the total amount transferred in a fiscal year cannot exceed $15 million (U.S.C. 2348a); direct drawdown of commodities and services from the inventory and resources of any agency of the U.S. government not to exceed $25 million in fiscal year (U.S.C. 2348a); President may carry out drawdowns valued at up to $300 million per year. Up to $100 million of this amount may be drawn from DoD for unspecified emergencies that require immediate military assistance (Sec. 506 of FAA, subsection 506a1).	http://www.dsca. osd.mil/programs/ biz-ops/drawdown_ handbook_2004b.pdf
International Narcotics Control and Law Enforcement Program (INCLE) better known as (INL),	Training on nonlethal techniques Equipment	FAA, Sec. 481	Provide counternarcotics related training to foreign military and law enforcement personnel. Program includes the purchase of defense articles, services and training.	www.usaid.gov/policy/ads/ faa.pdf
Andean Counterdrug Initiative (Plan Colombia)	Training on lethal and nonlethal techniques Equipment	P.L. 106-246	$45,000,000 shall be available for the provision of support for counterdrug activities of the government of Colombia.	http://asafm.army. mil/Documents/ OtherDocuments/CongInfo/ BLDL/PL//00ESUPpl.pdf

Program	Categories	Authority	Language	Source Link
Enhanced Int'l Peacekeeping Capabilities (EIPC) Initiative (now subsumed by GPOI)	Training on nonlethal techniques Equipment	No law governs EIPC; a policy initiative combining resources from FMF (AECA Sec. 23 & S24); FMET (FAA Sec. 541); EDA (FAA Sec. 541); Joint Military Exercises (10 U.S.C.)	In September 1996, the National Security Council endorsed the Enhanced International Peacekeeping Capabilities (EIPC) concept as a means to focus U.S. government resources on the improvement of selected nations' peacekeeping capabilities. The EIPC initiative is a peacetime engagement tool designed to help increase the pool of armed forces capable of participating in multinational peace support operations.	http://www.ccmr.org/ public/library_file_proxy. cfm/lid/1860/f/eipc_info_ paper.pdf
Global Train and Equip Program	Equipment Training on lethal and nonlethal techniques	National Defense Authorization Act 2006 or 2007; P.L. 109-163	Train and equip foreign military forces for two purposes. One is to enable such forces to perform counterterrorism operations. The other is to enable foreign military forces to participate in or to support military and stability operations in which U.S. armed forces participate. Authorized to provide equipment, supplies, and training to foreign country to increase capacity.	http://www.dod.mil/ dodgc/olc/docs/ PL109-163.pdf

Program	Categories	Authority	Language	Source Link
Operation Enduring Freedom– Trans Sahara	Equipment, security services	Pan Sahel Initiative, Trans Saharan Initiative	PSI is a State Department–led effort to assist Mali, Niger, Chad, and Mauritania in detecting and responding to suspicious movement of people and goods across and within their borders through training, equipment, and cooperation. Its goals support two U.S. national security interests in Africa: waging the war on terrorism and enhancing regional peace and security. Technical assessments taking place in each country will help focus training and other capacity-building resources over the coming months. PSI will assist participating countries to counter known terrorist operations and border incursions, as well as trafficking of people, illicit materials, and other goods. Accompanying the training and material support will be a program to bring military and civilian officials from the four countries together to encourage greater cooperation and information exchange within and among the regional governments on counterterrorism and border security.	http://www.africom.mil/oef-ts.asp

APPENDIX C

What Factors Influence the Shape and Assist (Option C) Mission?

An important question is how to characterize those circumstances in which some or all of the Shape and Assist (Option C) capabilities described in Chapter Five would be needed. Important considerations include

- the existence, size, and strength of an insurgency
- the geography (size, borders, terrain, etc.) of the host nation
- the capabilities of the host nation
  - government competence and openness
  - size, quality, loyalty, and culture of the host nation's security force
- U.S. national interests and policies.

Below, we address each of these considerations in turn, drawing on secondary source information on insurgencies in Vietnam, El Salvador, and Colombia.

Character of the Insurgency

The existence, size, and strength of an insurgency inevitably affect what U.S. security assistance can do for a partner country. For example, the FMLN insurgency proved resilient despite a large increase in U.S. military assistance to the Salvadoran government in the 1980s.[1] As COL Lyman C. Duryea, the defense attaché between 1983 and 1985, observed, "we have arrived at a point [in 1986] where additional infusions of training, materiel, and various other elements of security assistance won't move us toward the ultimate goal of defeating the insurgency, but will merely reinforce the stalemate."[2] In recent years, the Colombian government has faced three different, albeit interrelated, insurgencies: the FARC, the paramilitaries, and the National Liberation Army (ELN). Of the two main adversaries, the paramilitaries have targeted civil society, whereas the FARC has tended to attack representatives of the state.[3] Despite recent setbacks, the FARC, the ELN, and the paramilitaries are made up of seasoned fighters. Moreover, the FARC has had a very different experience from that of the FMLN in El Salva-

---

[1] Montgomery, p. 42.

[2] Montgomery, p. 44.

[3] Julia Sweig, "What Kind of War for Colombia?" *Foreign Affairs,* Vol. 81, No. 5, 2002.

dor, which may make the former rebel group less amenable to a negotiated political settlement with government forces.[4]

Host Nation Geography

The geography of host nation can influence the severity of a conflict and the skills needed to contain it. Colombia provides an example of challenges that could be addressed by SC/TAA programs and efforts. Colombia is three times the size of California and 53 times the size of El Salvador.[5] Venezuela shares a border with Colombia about as long as that between the United States and Mexico. Historically, Venezuela and Colombia have been relatively good neighbors. More recently, however, Colombia has accused Venezuela's president, Hugo Chavez, of supporting the FARC and the ELN.[6] Although Peru's border with Colombia is about half the size of Venezuela's and well secured, it is not clear that Peru perceives the eradication of Colombia coca, which could drive cultivation back to Peru, as being in its national interest.[7]

Capabilities of Host Nation Government

Government competence and openness affects the likelihood that U.S. military assistance will achieve success. Robust political-military efforts are often called for when there are significant government shortcomings. Centrist civilian governments in El Salvador turned out to be a weak reed on which to pin U.S. hopes for reform since the antireform military held most of the power. El Salvador's civilian bureaucracy lacked the military's capacity to plan, implement, and coordinate programs, not to mention its access to guns. For its part, the U.S. foreign assistance bureaucracy lacked the ability to help strengthen the capacity and unity of effort of Salvadoran civil bureaucracies.[8]

Colombia's central government historically has been weak in terms of presence outside the major cities and in terms of major government functions.[9] For example, upward of 95 percent of crimes in Colombia are never prosecuted; tax collection hovers at approximately 10 percent of GDP, half the U.S. rate; conscription laws enable the children of the elite to avoid fighting in the army; and the defense budget remains significantly lower than that of other countries in conflict and, for that matter, lower than that of other Latin American countries at peace.[10]

---

[4] Sweig, p. 136.

[5] Sweig, p. 136.

[6] Sweig, p. 137.

[7] Sweig, p. 138.

[8] Edwin G. Corr, "Societal Transformation for Peace in El Salvador," *Annals of the American Academy of Political and Social Science,* Vol. 541, September 1995, p. 155.

[9] Sweig, p. 125.

[10] Sweig, p. 133.

Capabilities of Host Nation Security Forces

The force size, quality, loyalty, and culture of the host nation will play a major role in determining what, if any, security cooperation programs a country will need. For example, the South Vietnamese military was thoroughly corrupt and politicized. U.S. MAAG-V advisors worked for years with an RVNAF that valued political reliability over military competence. Divided command with overlapping responsibilities, widespread corruption, and previous combat experience under the French had created a South Vietnamese officer corps where "few. . . shared, or even understood, the American officers' belief in coordination, team-work, loyalty to superiors and subordinates, know-how, and delegation of authority."[11]

The Salvadoran Army in the 1970s and early 1980s was poorly trained and equipped, brutal, unpopular, and deeply resistant to American imposed change. In 1981, the U.S. Southern Command's El Salvador Military Strategy Assistance Team indicated that the ESAF "has a remarkable capacity for tolerating unprofessional and improper conduct which does not threaten the institution."[12] The Salvadoran officer corps welcomed technical advice but resented criticism of basic military skills.[13] ESAF commanders particularly disliked the American emphasis on human rights and the Americans' "inclination to take charge in the face of inefficiency and ineptitude."[14] Salvadoran military leaders learned to tell Americans what they wanted to hear with respect to structural reform issues in order to get U.S. aid.[15] Therefore, although the 1980s saw an improvement of the Salvadoran armed forces in many respects, the civil war continued to be a stalemate with little chance of a military solution.[16]

U.S. and Host Nation Strategic Interests

U.S. interests and policy provide the framework in which SC/TAA takes place. At times, this framework places strategic interests in conflict with each other. The SAO will have to work within this framework and with these conflicts. For example, U.S. perception of its strategic interest was at odds with its human rights policy in El Salvador. Top ESAF leaders correctly perceived that the United States saw the outcome of the conflict in El Salvador as essential to U.S. interests. They were therefore able to completely ignore human rights pressures from the Carter administration.[17] The same is true today in Iraq.[18]

---

[11] Ramsey, p. 44.

[12] Ramsey, p. 85.

[13] Brian J. Bosch, *The Salvadoran Officer Corps and the Final Offensive of 1981,* Jefferson, North Carolina: McFarland & Co., 1999, p. 15.

[14] Ramsey, p. 96.

[15] Martin Diskin and Kenneth Sharpe, *The Impact of U.S. Policy in El Salvador, 1979–1985,* Berkeley, California: Berkeley Institute of International Studies, University of California, 1986, p. 21.

[16] Bosch, p. 112.

[17] William Deane Stanley, "El Salvador: State-Building Before and After Democratisation, 1980–95," *Third World Quarterly,* Vol. 27, No. 1, p. 102.

[18] Author's observation based on experience in the Coalition Provisional Authority and the U.S. embassy in Baghdad, 2004 and 2006–2007.

Some argue that congressional constraints on the provision of assistance to Colombia have hindered administration attempts to create a coherent TAA strategy. In the late 1980s, Congress enacted statutes that still constrain U.S. assistance to Colombia. For example, no equipment and training could go to Colombian forces for counterinsurgency missions, and no assistance could go to military units that harbored violators of human rights (Leahy Amendment). The latter created a lengthy and complex vetting process for all Colombian soldiers who receive U.S. assistance.[19] In early August 2002, Washington also requested a written statement from Bogotá conferring immunity on United States military advisers in Colombia as a precondition for the continuation of military aid.[20]

Since the administration of George H.W. Bush, U.S. officials have wrestled with balancing U.S. interest in drug eradication against local efforts to combat domestic insurgencies in Latin America.[21] According to the original Plan Colombia concept, economic development, security, and peace were inextricably linked. Reducing the flow of drug money decreased the military capacity of all three terrorist groups. Thus, there was a convergence of U.S. and Colombian strategic interests. However, the convergence was only partial.[22] Even though the training and equipping of counternarcotics battalions easily transferred to other units, it did not have much impact on the larger army. Furthermore, there was a danger that creating separate capabilities for counternarcotics and other military missions would weaken coordination among the Colombian armed forces, the Colombian antinarcotics battalions, and U.S. military advisors.[23]

---

[19] Gabriel Marcella, *The United States and Colombia: the Journey from Ambiguity to Strategic Clarity,* Carlisle Barracks, Pa.: Strategic Studies Institute, U.S. Army War College, 2003, p. 51.

[20] Tickner, p. 85.

[21] Sweig, pp. 127–128.

[22] Marcella, p. 39.

[23] Marcella, p. 56.

Bibliography

Andrade, Dale, and LCOL James H. Willbanks, "CORDS/Phoenix: Counterinsurgency Lessons from Vietnam for the Future," *Military Review*, March–April 2006.

Arms Export Control Act of 1976 (P.L. 94–329), Section 23.

Bart, Mark Henniker, "The Emergency in Malaya, 1948–60," *Journal of the Royal Central Asian Society*, Vol. 51, No. 1, 1964, pp. 37–38.

Bosch, Brian J., *The Salvadoran Officer Corps and The Final Offensive of 1981*, Jefferson, N.C.: McFarland & Co., 1999.

Coffey, MAJ Ross, "Revisiting CORDS: The Need for Unity of Effort to Secure Victory in Iraq," *Military Review*, March–April 2006.

Corr, Edwin G., "Societal Transformation for Peace in El Salvador," *Annals of the American Academy of Political and Social Science*, Vol. 541, September 1995, p. 144.

Defense Institute for Security Assistance Management (DISAM), *Green Book*, undated. As of July 10, 2008: http://www.disam.dsca.mil/pubs/DR/greenbook.htm

Department of Defense, "Military Support for Stability, Security, Transition, and Reconstruction Operations," DoD Directive 3000.05, November 28, 2005.

———, *Quadrennial Defense Review Report*, February 2006.

———, *Interagency, Intergovernmental Organization, and Nongovernmental Organization Coordination During Joint Operations*, Joint Publication 3-08, March 17, 2006.

———, *Department of Defense Operations at U.S. Embassies*, DoD Directive 5105.75, December 21, 2007.

Diskin, Martin, and Kenneth Sharpe, *The Impact of U.S. policy in El Salvador, 1979–1985*, Berkeley, Calif.: Berkeley Institute of International Studies, University of California, 1986.

Donnelly, BGEN Edward P., Deputy Director, G-35, Headquarters, Department of the Army, "Army Approach to Security Force Assistance," unpublished briefing, September 2, 2009.

Feickert, Andrew, *U.S. Military Operations in the Global War on Terrorism: Afghanistan, Africa, the Philippines, and Colombia*, Washington, D.C.: Congressional Research Service, February 4, 2005.

Foreign Assistance Act of 1986, P.L. 99-529, Section 660.

Freedom Support Act of 1992, P.L. 102-511.

Headquarters, Department of the Army, *Operations*, FM 3-0, February 2008.

———, *Security Force Assistance*, FM 3-07-1, May 2009.

Isacson, Adam, "Optimism, Pessimism, and Terrorism: The United States and Colombia in 2003," *Brown Journal of World Affairs*, Vol. 10, No. 2, Spring 2004.

Joint Chiefs of Staff, *Department of Defense Dictionary of Military and Associated Terms*, Joint Publication 1-02, June 9, 2004.

———, *Doctrine for Joint Special Operations*, Joint Publication 3-05, December 17, 2003.

Komer, Robert W., *Bureaucracy Does Its Thing: Institutional Constraints on U.S.-GVN Performance in Vietnam*, Santa Monica, Calif.: RAND Corporation, R-967-ARPA, 1972. As of October 9, 2009: http://www.rand.org/pubs/reports/R967/index.html

Manwaring, Max G., and Court Prisk, eds., *El Salvador and War: An Oral History of Conflict from the 1979 Insurrection to the Present*, Washington, D.C.: National Defense University Press, 1988.

Marcella, Gabriel, *The United States and Colombia: The Journey from Ambiguity to Strategic Clarity*, Carlisle Barracks, Pa.: Strategic Studies Institute, U.S. Army War College, 2003.

Menendez, Senator Robert, "U.S. Foreign Assistance Under the Microscope at Senate Hearing," press release, June 12, 2007. As of November 30, 2009: http://menendez.senate.gov/newsroom/press/release/?id=84a494a9-745f-4727-adae-f5f4ef805127

Montgomery, Tommie Sue, "Fighting Guerrillas: The United States and Low-Intensity Conflict in El Salvador," *New Political Science*, Vol. 9, No. 18–19, Autumn 1990.

Nagl, John A., *Learning to Eat Soup with a Knife*, Chicago, Ill.: University of Chicago Press, 2002.

———, *Institutionalizing Adaptation: It's Time for a Permanent Army Advisory Corps*, Center for a New American Security, June 2007.

National Defense Authorization Act of 2007, P.L. 109-163, Section 1206.

Ramsey, Robert D. III, *Advising Indigenous Forces: American Advisors in Korea, Vietnam, and El Salvador*, Global War on Terrorism Occasional Paper 18, Fort Leavenworth, Kan.: Combat Studies Institute Press, 2006.

Robert T. Stafford Disaster Relief and Emergency Assistance Act, P.L. 93-288, as amended, 42 U.S.C. 5121-5207, November 23, 1988.

Simpson, Erin M., "The Country Team in Laos, 1965–1973," *The Country Team in American Strategy*, unpublished manuscript, December 2006.

Stanley, William Deane, "El Salvador: State-Building Before and After Democratisation, 1980–95," *Third World Quarterly*, Vol. 27, No. 1, pp. 101–114.

Support for Eastern European Democracies (SEED) Act of 1989, P.L. 101-179.

Sweig, Julia, "What Kind of War for Colombia?" *Foreign Affairs*, Vol. 81, No. 5, 2002, pp. 122–141.

Tickner, Andrew B., "Colombia and the United States: From Counternarcotics to Counterterrorism," *Current History*, February 2003.

Unger, Noam, "Foreign Assistance Reform: Then, Now, and Around the Bend," *InterAction*, July 2007. As of June 1, 2008: http://www.brookings.edu/~/media/Files/rc/articles/2007/07foreignassistance_unger/200707unger.pdf

Waghelstein, John D., "Ruminations of a Pachyderm or What I Learned in the Counter-Insurgency Business," *Small Wars and Insurgencies*, Vol. 5, No. 3, Winter 1994.

Wallace, William S., "FM 3-0 Operations: The Army's Blueprint," *Military Review*, March–April 2008.